=== *The* ===

Inside Track

TOM COURTNEY

PAGE PUBLISHING, INC.
New York, NY

First originally published by Page Publishing, Inc. 2018

ISBN 978-1-64298-497-2 (Paperback)
ISBN 978-1-64298-500-9 (Digital)

Printed in the United States of America

M y thanks go to my wife, Posy L'Hommedieu Courtney, for encouraging me to write the many stories she had heard over our fifty-five years of marriage. She said I should write this for our grandchildren and other young people.

I hope some of these stories might be an inspiration to young people to know they can go their own way—let them know that life has many unusual twists and turns, but with persistence and determination, things can work out.

I hope all of my friends will enjoy my experiences. I am sure they will discover some of these stories will have surprise endings. Hence the title of my book, *The Inside Track*.

CONTENTS

CHAPTER 1

Growing Up in Livingston, New Jersey

I was a baseball player—a pitcher. My dad, James Courtney, was a pitcher and had signed with the Yankees in 1928. Babe Ruth and Lou Gehrig were Yankees in 1928. In 1929 The Depression hit and James Courtney married Dolores Goerdes in 1929, and they had their first child, James Jr., in 1930. In the off-season, Dad got a job with the Lackawanna Railroad to support his family. (In those days, almost all the players had to have full-time jobs in the off-seasons.) Dad had to give up baseball.

My oldest brother, Jim, was a power hitter; second brother Brian was an excellent infielder born in 1932. I was the third brother in 1933. Dennis, number four in 1935, was a great catcher, and Kevin, born in 1950, was a surprise addition to the family. He was also an excellent ballplayer.

Baseball was the family game. My GrandPa Tom, pitched for The Scranton, Pennsylvania team and beat Christy Mathewson 1 to 0 in 1893. As we grew up in Livingston, New Jersey, we played a lot of baseball. I was the poorest baseball player of the brothers.

My godfather, Billy Stanton, was Dad's first cousin. He fought Pete Latzo twice for the world lightweight title in the 1920s. He lost both times, but he won almost all of his one hundred fights. Billy would drive up from Orange, New Jersey, to give us weekly boxing lessons. We were good boxers and rarely lost a fight that someone else started.

One time when Billy was driving up to Livingston to give us his weekly boxing lesson, he inadvertently got in the way of a truck driver. The truck driver raced up and forced Billy's car off the road. He got out and opened Billy's car door and pulled him out. By the time Billy's feet hit the ground, he had hit the truck driver with six punches.

Each punch had cut the guy's face before the truck driver collapsed on the ground. The truck driver took Billy before the Orange, New Jersey, judge claiming Billy had used a wrench on him. The truck driver weighed 220 pounds, was 6'4", and in his twenties. Billy weighed 120 pounds and was 75 years old. The judge, who had known Billy for many years, asked to see his hands. They were still badly cut. He told Billy his hands were a lethal weapon and would not tolerate him fighting again. He told the truck driver he should throw him in jail for picking on a little old man. The brothers were very impressed with their boxing coach. I tell this story because it represented how my parents thought about life. You had an obligation in life to do the best you could, to use God's graces as gifts to help in life's journey. Be willing to take risks, but always be willing to give more than you expect to receive. Don't start a fight, but finish it. Persistence and determination were the obligations of life.

Livingston, New Jersey, was a great town. We had a gym a block from our house, and the recreation director, Mr. Andehazy, had a different program almost every night of the week. I went the first six grades to a school that was three quarters of a mile from home. My brother, Brian, and I used to run to school, run home for lunch, and run home after school. My Dad encouraged us not to ride the school bus, unless the weather was bad.

At Fourth of July, we would compete at the town picnic for prizes. For about two weeks, my mother would have us practice all the events—running races, high jump, long jump, three-legged race, and sack races. We came home with a lot of prizes.

Tom "The Look of Determination"

CHAPTER 2

High School: Leaving Baseball for Track

In my freshman year at Caldwell High School, I went out for the freshman baseball team. I kept hoping I would get cut, but because my two older brothers were such good players, the coach kept me on the team. As a sophomore, I again went out for junior varsity hoping I would get cut, but I made the team. I played very little as a substitute pitcher. One day the coach, Mr. Tierney, got up in practice to hit against me. I hit him twice. (I had a good fast ball.) He benched me. I asked him if I was going to play again. He said I had a good fast ball, but poor control. I suggested he had poor reflexes. I went back to the bench but decided I would try another sport in my junior year. I played varsity basketball, and the basketball coach, Dwight Burr, was the new field coach for the track and field team.

He said he had heard I was going out for another sport. He suggested I try the pole vault. He said I was tall, strong, and fast. These were the very things I needed to be a good pole vaulter. I had decided I liked the idea of playing tennis, but after watching the boys on the tennis team for fifteen minutes, I could see they were very good and it would take lot of time to get up to that level. I thought I would give the pole vault a try. When I arrived at the track, the head coach, Emil Piel, our physics teacher, asked me what I was doing. I told him

I was going to try the pole vault. He said he had watched me in gym for several years and I would make a very good runner. He said he was about to start an inter-squad half-mile race. He wanted me to hop into the race and see how I would do. I did. I ended up winning. I never became a pole vaulter.

I started track as a junior at Caldwell High. I lost my first race to Les Wallach of Blair Academy in 2:07. I won the next few races before I ran in the Newark Invitational. The final was one race with about forty to fifty participants. I got tangled at the start, and got knocked down. I got up, with some spike wounds, and did move from down 40 yards to sixth in the race. I ran and won several dual meets and won our conference meet in 2:05. We went to the state meet at Rutgers University. I was running against an outstanding runner named Ray Wheiler. Fred Dwyer, a super high school miler at Seton Hall Prep, was at Villanova. He talked to me about Villanova's interest in me. (He was also recruiting Ray Wheiler.) Fred told me if I would lead Wheiler for the first quarter, he would be discouraged and he might give up the race. He set a new national high school record of 1:54. He ran the first 440 in 50 seconds, 4 seconds faster than I had ever run in a 440. I took third in the race. Ray went to Villanova with Fred Dwyer.

In my senior year, my father convinced me to run from the front to avoid collisions. In the Newark Invitational, I ran out and built a 40-yard lead. With a half lap to go, I started to tire and lost 39 of those 40 yards, but won the race. I remained undefeated the rest of the track season. I won the fastest half mile in the state meet held at Rutgers University in 1951 with a time of 2 minutes.

1953 one of Tom's many summer jobs,
Good Humor and Life Guard

Life Guard

College Years

After my race at the New Jersey state meet, Artie O'Conner, the Fordham University coach, came up to me. He said, "Tom, you have the potential to be an outstanding runner at Fordham." He offered me a full scholarship. When my mother heard this, she was so excited. Her favorite cousin, Charlie Deubel, had gone to Fordham and became captain of the track team.

I had taken the New Jersey test for a tuition scholarship at the University of Pennsylvania, and the school called and told me I had taken second. Shortly thereafter they called and said the student that had won decided to go to Harvard, and would I like to take his place. I said yes.

Ken Daugherty was the head coach at Penn. He knew I had won the New Jersey scholarship for academics. I was naive and too shy to ask for a full scholarship. Yale coach Bob Geigengack offered me tuition, but when I said I also needed room and board, he told me how wonderful Yale was but did not come back to me. Several other colleges offered me full deals, including Villanova and Georgetown.

I had decided to go to Fordham. I never saw the school until the day before classes started. I arrived with my dad and one suitcase (the very heavy alligator thing that my dad bought when he made the Yankees). One young man named Bill Condren, who was in the registration room, asked if he could carry my suitcase up to my room. I assumed he was an upper classmate making a few dollars. He refused my attempted tip.

The next day I went to class and there was Bill Condren sitting next to me. Two weeks later, I saw he was running for freshman class president. I convinced several of my new friends to vote for Bill. He won. He ran for president in his senior year but lost.

I went over to the gymnasium and the track coach, Artie O'Conner, took a group of us over to Van Cortland Park to run through the hills. I never had run more than a half mile. Bill Persicetty, a sophomore and Jersey boy, was on the varsity cross-country team. He had run at St. Peter's Prep and had been the New Jersey half-mile champ a year earlier. Bill said he would take me for a practice run. We ran three miles and Percy was right alongside of me, urging me to stay up with him. We ran under 16 minutes for three miles. I was ready to collapse. That was the fastest time I ran on the freshman cross-country squad for the cross-country season. It took me several days to recover.

When we started the indoor season, we ran our first practice in the gym. Bill Persicetty came over to coach Artie O'Conner and said he would like to do a half mile with the "New Jersey state champion." Again he ran me into the ground. My time was the fastest I had ever run, but Bill was a little faster. I was exhausted and it took several days to recover.

Some weeks later we had tryouts for the two-mile relay. I ran 1.56, my best time ever, and made the team. I went to the dining room for dinner and passed out.

The school put me in the infirmary, where I stayed for about two weeks. They released me. I asked if I could go back to practice. They said yes. I went over to see Coach O'Conner. He said great, and they were going to have another time trial for the two-mile relay team. I ran the trial in 1.56, duplicating my best time ever. I went back to dinner and passed out again.

I went back into the infirmary for a few more weeks. They didn't know what was wrong with me. They released me and said I could run again.

Still I felt exhausted but went back to the practice track. One major problem was my roommate, Paul Finn. He rocked his bed every other minute when he slept, and it was noisy. I taped his bed springs, I oiled them and stuffed them with cotton, but they still were noisy. Also Paul took a nap every afternoon while I was at track practice. He stayed up late every night. Paul was a nice person but not a good roommate for me. He also had friends in our room after I went to bed. One night a football player was in my room at 1 a.m. I asked him to leave so I could get some sleep. He said, "Screw you." I jumped out of bed, picked him up, and fired him through the open door. He was so stunned that he got up and—to my astonishment and disbelief—left.

I should have been smart enough to get out of that situation, but at home we were taught to do the best we could with what we had. Also I was carrying 18 credits, including ROTC classes and remedial religion. Most of the boys in my class had gone to Catholic schools before going to Fordham and with tests were exempt from those classes.

I also had to go to the 7:30 a.m. Mass, then wait tables for breakfast. Scholarship students had to wait breakfast tables until they were on the dean's list. That meant my other classmates went to the 8:00 a.m. Mass. It was a real incentive because after the first quarter, I never waited tables again.

I realized later that I had become so exhausted that I wound up with mononucleosis.

I ran again but had lost my strength and ran poorly for several months. I was considering dropping track. I finished my first year. My Dad picked me up with my alligator suitcase and took me home. He fed me steaks, and I slept late for several weeks.

He said, "Okay, Tom, you are looking good and I would like you to try running in the New Jersey AAU Championship." I trained that week and on Saturday ran and won the half mile in 1.55—the best time I had ever run.

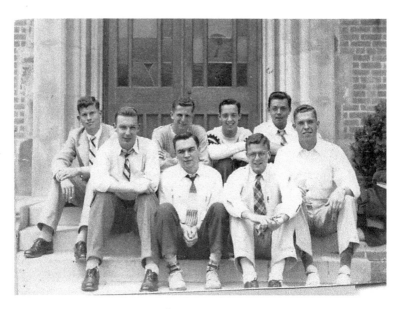

Fordham roommates

l to r back row: Ruppert Wentworth,
Bob Mackin, Steve Huben, Carl Candel

l to r front row: Jack Dash, Jack Stanton,
Bob Malone, Tom Courtney

When I was going back to Fordham for my second year, Coach O'Conner called and said he had decided not to have me run cross-country. He suggested I work out in the Bronx Botanical Gardens. The gardens were next door to Fordham and alongside the Bronx Zoo. It was a great place to train.

I moved in with a new roommate named Ruppert Wentworth. He was also a 440 runner on the track team. With my new roommate, who was a very considerate young man, it was a good year. I ended up taking second place in the half mile in the Metropolitan Championship. Lou Jones beat me by a narrow margin, 1.52. Lou later broke the 400-meter world record in the 1955 Pan American Games in Mexico City.

Cover for IC4A, Tom's first major win 2.10.

Tom is on the right, winning.

In my junior year, I became the IC4A 1000-yard indoor record holder. Paul Raudenbush from Penn was second, and Mike Stanley from Yale was third.

The coach of Penn pulled me aside one night after we beat the Penn two-mile relay team by about a foot. "Gosh," Ken Dougherty said, "just think what a relay team we would have if you had come to Penn. What made you decide to go to Fordham?" I said, "Three things. One was the public trolley cars inside the campus. Two, the room I was to get at Penn had pieces of paint hanging from the ceiling (I did not know that was collegiate at the time), and three, when you introduced me to the president of Penn, Harold Stassen (who had run for president of the United States seven times), he said, "I hope you can run fast because they really hit hard out there."

During my junior year, I fell in love with Pat O'Driscol from New Rochelle College. I couldn't breathe when I was with her.

1955 NYAC had a great squad and won
the National Championships

I ran in the National AAU Championships in St. Louis with my NYAC squad. Unfortunately we went to St. Louis University track for a workout. It was closed with a six-foot spiked fence around it. It didn't faze us. We climbed over it and took our workout. After a hard workout, and somewhat tired, I slipped on the top of the fence and one of the steel spikes went right into my calf. I pulled it off the fence and luckily fell on the outside of the fence. I went to the hospital and there was a question if I would run.

Two days later on Friday, I ran the semi-final and won my heat in 1.49. In the final the next evening, I was lined up next to Mal Whitfield. There was a general false start.

Next Whitfield made a fake move, and I stepped out over the starting line. I was disqualified. From that day, I started with a sprinter's start, rather than my previous standing start.

I went home and worked all summer at the Livingston Water Department as I had done for several summers. We dug holes in the streets for new fireplugs and new water and sewer hook-ups. I liked the eight hours of digging and was able to do 100 push-ups and 50 chin-ups at the end of the summer. I also did some running with my brother, Brian. He would run the first lap of a three-quarter-mile run, drop out for a lap, then challenge me on the third lap.

One day Brian, my brother, said to me, "Tom, you are a poor dancer."

I said, "Brian, you are worse." He said he had seen an advertisement to learn to be an Arthur Murray dance instructor. We both signed up. After the first week, they saw Brian had a severe case of poison ivy and told him he was being dropped. They told me I was also being dropped. This was on Friday afternoon. I said I hadn't shown how good I was, and wanted to come in on Monday for a trial. Over the weekend I practiced 12 hours a day. When I had my trial, they were stunned that I was so good. I finished the program and started giving lessons. I told them I had to go back to Fordham College. They said that was fine and that they had a studio on Fordham Road and I could give lessons there. I said I hoped I could get some time and would let them know.

I went back for my senior year and invited Pat O'Driscol to our first school dance. The band played the usual foxtrot, and changed to the cha-cha. Pat went to sit down. I said it was too bad you don't know how to do these dances. She said she did all those dances, but didn't think I could do them. She was a good dancer. We did the rumba, tango, waltz, charleston, and the cha-cha. She said she had no idea that I was such an excellent dancer. I never told her about my Arthur Murray lessons.

In my junior year, I ran the outdoor IC4A Championship and a slender half-miler from the University of Pittsburgh named Arnie Sowell ran past me with a lap to go. I thought I should run up and pass him. I was so sure I could get him with my kick that I waited. When we came down the final straight away, he outsprinted me. I actually heard my mother in the stands. "He can't lose," she said. I heard my brother, Jim, say, "He can and he just did."

In my senior year, I lost a number of races, including the National Indoor Championship, to Arnie Sowell. In that race Sowell set a new world 1000 record. Audun Boysen from Norway took second. He was the European champion. I took third. The papers the next day carried Boysen's quote: "Take care of Sowell. He is your next Olympic champion."

Two weeks later the track coaches at their track luncheon were telling what event their runners were going to run in the IC4A'a. My coach, Artie C'Conner, put me in the 600 instead of my usual event, the 1000. He said, "I think Tom would have a chance to win that event. What's the point of having him run for second in the 1000 behind Sowell." George Eastman, the coach of Manhattan, said that Arnie Sowell was the greatest, most fabulous runner who ever lived. He said Sowell could win the 1000, but also if he wanted the 600, the mile, and even the two-mile.

When I saw this in the paper the next day, I was very disappointed. My own coach had given up on me. I was so upset that I could hardly sleep. Artie had always been my great supporter. I could hardly work out that week and ended up losing the 600 to Charlie Jenkins of Villanova. Suddenly I had this unexpected, out-of-the-blue, amazing feeling. I made a decision that I would beat Sowell. I ran every workout with a new dedication that I did not understand myself. I was going to beat Arnie Sowell and prove Coach O'Conner wrong.

We ran at the Penn Relays in my junior year. Our main competitor was Villanova. Freddy Dwyer, the famous miler, was running the anchor leg. When I received the baton from Bill Persicetty, we were 10 yards ahead. I ran hard and increased that lead.

The year before Villanova had run and won the two-mile famous relay in the Coliseum Relays. They were invited to come back the next year.

Jumbo Elliot, the coach of Villanova, told the meet promoters of the Coliseum Relays that they should instead invite Fordham because they had beaten his team at the Penn Relays. I always felt that Coach Elliot did us a tremendous favor and I never forgot it.

We were invited and there were 70,000 fans in the stadium. Terry Foley ran the first leg, and we were there at the next leg. Frank Tarsney ran one of his best races, and Bill Persicetty made up several yards on his leg. I was in third place, but only a few feet from the front. Michigan was second, and California, with Lon Spurrier, was in the lead. I ran the fastest race of my life and had one of my best finishing kicks. We won and that was exciting. We had no idea that we broke the world record with a time of 7.27. The record had been set by the previous Olympic team at 7.29. The anchor leg on that team was run by Mal Whitfield, who had won the 800 meters in the 1948 and 1952 Olympics.

1954 Fordham's Two Mile Relay Team
breaks the World Record 7.27.

Terry Foley, Frank Tarsney, Bill Persicetty, Tom Courtney

We had a good group at Fordham, and the relays were very important to our coach, Artie C'Conner. I was enjoying the relays. That is where I wanted to be.

My new time as anchor of the new world record was 1.48. Lou Miller, the writer at the *World Telegram*, wrote that my time was faster than Mal Whitfield's time for the world record, and he wanted to see us race one another. (Later in the 1956 Olympic Trials we did!)

In the spring of my senior year, I was in exceptional shape. We were training hard for the Penn Relays. As I was sprinting around the track, I stepped on a rock that had worked its way to the surface during the spring. I went down hard. I had severely twisted my ankle.

Coach O'Conner thought I had broken my ankle and immediately took me to the doctor. The doctor said it wasn't broken, but was a very bad sprain. He wanted to put a cast on it. I asked how long would the cast be on. He said ten to twelve weeks—in other words, until the end of my spring season. I called my father at work. He said, do not allow the doctor to put a cast on it. He said he was sending my brother, Dennis, to the doctor's office to bring me home. My dad had been Billy Stanton's trainer and was extraordinary in using massage and stretching to help heal sprains and other problems. When Dad got home that night, he worked it for hours and put ice on it. In the morning and every evening he worked on it. Two weeks later, he taped it and I ran in the Penn Relays. The ankle was still swollen and very sore. But a few weeks after that, I won the National Collegiate half-mile championship. (Sowell had gotten trapped in a slow heat and did not qualify for the final.) I ended up with a time that qualified me for the Olympic Trials. I also won the AAU meet, and qualified for a trip to Finland, Norway, Denmark, and Germany during the summer.

CHAPTER 4

Sugar Bowl and Wes Santee

I was invited to run in the 1955 Super Bowl 440-yard run in New Orleans. We were to run the day before the football game. That day it started to rain. Wes Santee, the great American miler, said he wanted to wait to run until the next day. I told him the forecast was for torrential rains the next day. He insisted and the organizers agreed to run the meet the next day. It poured and we ran with 4 inches of water on the track. No one did anything. I went out to the airport to catch my flight. Wes Santee and his wife, Diana, were there. Their flight had been cancelled due to the weather. My flight was about to leave when Wes came up to me and asked if I would give up my seat for his wife. She was pregnant, and he didn't want her to sleep on the hard airport floor. I didn't want to do it, but I agreed. They went to get her on my flight. The flight left and she came back into the airport. She said Wes took my ticket because he felt he couldn't miss tomorrow's workout. I slept on the floor that night next to his pregnant wife.

Later Wes Santee, Parry O' Brian, and J. W. Mashburn were accused of taking too much expense money by the AAU. O'Brian said if he did take too much expense money that he was going on a trip and he would return the $2.00 a day they gave him for spending money and that as soon as his mother got a job, she had agreed to help pay for the problem. J. W. Mashburn said the same.

Wes Santee said, "You Pharisees. You had sold 6000 tickets for the meet in Texas. I agreed to run and try to break the four-minute mile. The meet sold an additional 60,000 seats. What will you do with that money, drink wine for the next twenty years?"

The AAU said, "Wes, you are now a professional."

He said there is no professional track. They said, "That's right. You are it."

Wes was in the Marine Corp when the Olympic Trials were being held. He could run in the All-Service Championships. Wes had held the half-mile record, so he had qualified for the final in the 800 meters. Before the race, he came up to me and said this was the last 800 he would ever run and it would mean a great deal to him to win this race.

I looked at him in disbelief and remembered the Sugar Bowl stunt he had pulled on me. I said, "Under my breath, you will never win *this* race."

Coming off the final turn, Wes had the lead. As I ran past him in the stretch, he grabbed my arm. I yanked it away from him and ran to the finish line. As Lon Spurrier came by Wes, Wes tackled him into the infield. He refused to lose his last half-mile race.

Two days later, the buses were being filled. One to go to the Coliseum in Los Angeles for the AAU championships the next week; the other buses to take the service runners back to their bases. Wes was to go back to Quantico. Wes got on my bus and sat down next to me. He said it had been his life's ambition to run in the Olympics. Now that he wasn't going, he would place his hopes with me. They called for Wes to get off our bus, but instead he put his arms around me and started to cry. Several Marines MPs got on the bus and carried him off.

At that point I did feel sorry for him. He had an unbalanced view on life and was willing to do almost anything to achieve his goals. Despite that empathy, I did not like him.

My First Trip to Europe

It was a great thing as it was my first time on a trip. Since I won the nationals, I had my choice of trips with five other guys and coach Frank Potts from Colorado. The team included John Bennett, a 26-foot-long jumper; Bob Backus, the world record holder in the 35-pound weight throw; Bob Sieman, 1500 meters; Ken Reisner, 3000-meter steeplechase; Jack Yerman, 400 meters. I took the trip to Finland, Norway, Sweden, Germany, and a couple of other countries that first time. I ran thirty-five races in forty-five days. You didn't have to worry about training and basically didn't have to practice because we raced so often. It helped me and I ran against a lot of great runners over there and it was an experience that was important. The Finns were avid track fans. Paavo Nurmi had been a superstar, a holder of many world records in the mile and up.

Finland took credit for me going to the Olympics. I ran against the best Finnish runner, Dan Wern, as well as the Norwegian Audun Boyson, and the Danish champion Gunnar Nielson. In one of my last races that summer, I ran against Nielson. I decided to go for the world record. Running all the way from the front rarely was a good idea. I felt good and went out fast. I hit 49 seconds for the first 400. At 600 I ran 1.13 (4 seconds under the world record pace). With 50 meters to the finish, I had a 25-meter lead—then I died. Nielson nipped me at the tape. Our time was 146.8. That was 2/10 second off the world record of Rudolf Harbig. Harbig of Germany had died in World War II. To lose 25 meters in the last 50 meters was an agonizing defeat. I felt I had a limited number of opportunities. I had a great runner like Nielsen in the race, and he would inspire me.

Team on First Trip to Finland

L to R Dick Blair, Bobby Sieman, Tom Courtney, Ken Reisner, John Bennett, Bob Backus,

Coach Frank Potts.

In Finland I beat Audun Boyson, the 800 meter
European Champion, in a 1.46.2.
Third was the Finnish Champion Lassie Viron.

CHAPTER 6

You're in the Army Now

When I got back home I was drafted in the Army. I had been in the Air Force ROTC. In my last year, the Air Force said you had to fly to get a commission. I could not pass the eye test. I could go for three years as a sergeant in the Air Force, or two years as a private in the Army. Colonel Hull was in charge of recruiting track athletes with Olympic qualifying times for the Army. He promised me if I went into the Army, I would be given sufficient time to train for the Olympics. I decided to go in the Army.

When I arrived at Fort Dix, a sergeant said he was going to select squad leaders who would be in a private room versus the giant barracks room. He had each man step forward and tell if he had previous military experience. The first man said he had been in the Army Reserve. He was assigned squad leader. The next man said he was in the ROTC. He was told to get back in the line. I stepped forward and said, "Reserve Officers Training." The sergeant said "squad leader."

Some weeks later, I asked the master sergeant to see the commanding officer, Captain Hershall. The Sargent said, "What for?" I explained that Colonel Hull had promised that I would be given sufficient time to train for the Olympics and I was not getting that time. He said, "You jerk, you are in the Army now and I will let you know when you can see the captain." He did not.

A few nights later I was out taking my nightly run at 11 p.m. along the camp fence. It had some lights along it so I could see. Captain Hershall walked by and asked me what I was doing. I said I was training for the Olympics. He said, "Do you get up at 5 a.m. and spend the day training and go to bed at 10 p.m., but come out here at 11 p.m. to run?"

I said, "Yes, sir." He said, "Holy shit!" and walked away into the darkness. The next day we went out to bivouac to sleep in tents for a week. It was very cold. I mean very cold!

The next morning we got up at 5 a.m., and had breakfast. Next we were told to jump into a trench and throw a live grenade on command. The command was given, and I pulled the pin and jumped up and tried to throw the grenade. When I fell back in the trench, the grenade was stuck in my frozen hand. In a state of panic, I looked over to the other soldier who was with me in the trench. He screamed, "Throw it again." I again jumped up and threw it as hard as I could. The skin peeled off my hand, but so did the grenade. The other soldier was stark white, and I guess I was the same. They took me into the hospital truck and bandaged my hand. I was wondering what I would do next when I heard the sergeant call out, "Private Courtney, fall out for Olympic training at noon at the gym." The captain had sent me the orders. After training at the gym, I went back to the barracks. I was told that the truck would pick me up at 4 a.m. the next day and take me to my tent. I heard them coming the next morning, so I jumped under my bed and held myself up on the mattress springs so they could not see me. They left so I got back into bed and went back to sleep. At 11 a.m. the sergeant saw me and said, "Where the hell were you?" I said, "I was asleep and no one had called me." He said, "You are supposed to get out to the bivouac." He said to get in the truck, and they drove me out to bivouac. I had a quick lunch and jumped back into the truck and showed them my orders to train at the gym at 12 o'clock. It got so cold that bivouac was cancelled at the end of that day.

At the final physical tests of basic training, Captain Hershall came up to me and said he would appreciate it if I would score well in the six tests. I got a 100 in the first five tests. The sixth was jumping jacks, 100 in three minutes. I always avoided these because my college track coach said they were bad for runners, but I did them that day. I ended with a perfect score, the only one in the entire camp. That was on Monday, and I was to run the 1000-yard race at the Boston Garden on Friday. On Tuesday, I was so sore I could barely walk. On Wednesday, I could walk but not jog. On Thursday on my way up to Boston, I could jog, but not run. When they started the race on Friday, I managed to run. I was in last place for the first half of the race. Gradually I started to feel better and was sprinting at the finish for a photo-finish first place. The next day I sent Captain Hershall the newspaper photo of my race with a note saying, "Thank you for your help."

Next I was assigned to clerk typist school for advanced basic training. My bunk was next to Paul Zimmerman's, a football player from Columbia University who had a photographic memory and who was a great track fan. After my victory in Boston, I was excused weekends to run in Washington, Philadelphia, Boston, and New York track meets. The Army also gave me afternoons off to train for their meets. This meant that I had little time to learn my typing and the office procedures. At the end of the week, the entire group took an exam on Saturday, which included typing and fifty questions. When I would get back to the base on Sunday afternoon, Zim would tell me the fifty questions. The next morning the instructor would give me the test. As we finished our eight-week program, the head of the program was giving our awards. Finally he called me up and said I had the most unusual record for any past student. I scored 100 percent on the eight tests, the highest anyone had ever done, but when my typing was corrected, losing five points for every mistake, I ended up with an official five words per minute, one of the lowest scores on record. P.S. Paul Zimmerman went on to fame as a *Sports Illustrated* writer with an astounding record for predicting the outcome of the football games.

I had two other experiences in the Army that I can still vividly remember. As a squad leader, I slept in a side room with three other squad leaders and our assistant squad leaders. We had a regular Army sergeant that called us "Baby Soldiers." If there was any fooling around, or disturbance in the main bunk room of about one hundred recruits, you could hear his voice, "Okay, Baby Soldiers, you ten men will now go out on the parking lot and pick up cigarette butts. I don't want to see anything but elbows and assholes." One night when there was some noise, I slipped into the main barrack and said, in my best imitation, "Okay, Baby Soldiers, fall out to pick up cigarette butts." From the side came another voice, "Baby Soldier Private Courtney, go outside and pick up cigarette butts. I don't want to see anything but your elbows and asshole."

The other was just as we were finishing basic training, one of my friends in the squad told me they were going to give me a blanket party that night because I had been ordering them for eight weeks. (At a blanket party, a group covers you with a blanket, then beats the shit out of you.) I hid that night in a storage room, and they never found me. The next day it was my squad's turn to clean the latrine. When we got in there, one said they were all going to beat me up. I said I had tried to be fair and supportive and helpful all during basic training, but if they still wanted to fight me, I would fight them one at a time. Now there was one eighteen-year-old whom they called Animal. He was very strong and very big. He also had two giant teeth in the front of his mouth that were greatly loved by his mother. I told them then I wanted to fight Animal first, and they could decide who would be second. I said, "Animal, the first thing I am going to do is knock out your two front teeth and send them to your mother." Well, the pack pushed Animal forward, but Animal wilted back with his hands in front of his teeth. No one else volunteered to go second. That was an impending disaster that I shall never forget.

Use of Running Skills

Trip to Germany with Bob Rittenburg

We were on our way to Berlin to run in the NATO Games and decided to stay in a barracks to save money. At 5 a.m. the sergeant woke us to clean the latrine. We were prepared for such a problem. We had our bags packed and ready to go. As the sergeant said, "I'll show you where the cleaning materials are kept," we grabbed our bags and showed off our running skills. In a flash, we sailed out of the Army barracks and went to a hotel we had seen earlier that evening. We got up at noon and proceeded to the train station on our way to Berlin.

I also used my skills as a runner on a trip to Belgium. Bob Backus, a hammer thrower at 6'5", 230 pounds, also ran on our relay team when we needed him. We were walking in the town square when two attractive girls asked us to join them for a drink at one of the restaurants. We said okay but selected another restaurant about two blocks away. We wanted to be sure we were not part of a con game. They agreed and we went in and ordered some beers. The girls, however, ordered some wine (champagne). I sensed a problem and asked to see our bill at that point. The beers were okay, but the four champagnes were $25.00 a glass. In 1955 that would use up twenty-five days of our spending money. These girls and all the restaurants in the area were in on the con game. I said, "Bob, on the count of three." At three, we raced out the front door.

The next morning our coach was bemoaning the huge bill he had paid at one of the restaurants.

Three-Quarters of a Mile

When in the Army, I went to an Army meet in Texas and went over to work out at Houston University. Johnny Morris was the coach. I knew him because he had some good relay teams. He was pleased to have me work out with his runners. He asked me what I wanted to do. I told him I wanted to run a fast 1320 (three quarters of a mile) in about 2.56. We ran the first lap and he called out the 60 seconds. At the half, he said 2.00. I felt I had run better and tried to increase my pace. At the finish, he said, "Good run, Tom—2.52." He said I had done 58 for the first quarter, 1.55 for the half mile. He apologized for giving me the wrong times but said he knew his runners would drop out if they heard the actual times. I felt I could have gone on for another quarter that day and his trick had made me run 5 seconds faster than I had ever run for the three quarters of a mile. It also made me think about running the mile.

CHAPTER 7

Return of Ray Wheiler

As an aside I ran against Ray Wheiler in my junior year in a Fordham/Villanova dual meet. We didn't have half the size team as Villanova, so our coach asked us to double up in the meet. I agreed to run in the mile for third place, try to win the half mile, and come back on the mile relay team. Terry Foley was our top miler and won the event over John Joe Barry Villanova's miler from Ireland. I ran with the pack and took third place.

Ray Wheiler was a senior at Villanova, and the same runner who broke the national high school record of 1.54. He was in the half mile. I was told that Ray had lost interest in track and was barely breaking two minutes in the half mile. When Ray saw me, his interest changed and he ran a fierce race. I beat him at the tape in 1.49 (a track record.) I was exhausted from the mile and the half mile and told our coach I wouldn't do well in the mile relay. The coach had Ruppert Wentworth, my roommate at Fordham, run as my replacement. To this day I wish I had run the mile relay. Ruppert got excited and went out like a shot, built a big lead, and died in the last 50 yards. We lost the race and the meet.

The final chapter with Ray was yet to come. I ran on a sprint medley on a Fort Dix team in the Penn Relays. Charlie Pratt, a great friend and hurdler from Manhattan (and in 1958 was the World Decathlon Champion), was one of our men on our team. As he wrote in his book, *Many Villages Raised Charlie Pratt*, our anchorman was Tom Courtney, and I knew that if Tom was within 100 yards of the leader, he would catch him. Well, our first two legs, the 400 and the 220 were a disaster. What Charlie didn't know was the other service team had Ray Wheiler as anchor with a 60-yard lead. I knew that the key to my running was to relax and let my legs do the flying. I used to call it freewheeling. I took off and by the end of the first lap, I had cut the lead to 30 yards. We came down the final straight away and I was ten yards back. I kept barreling down to the finish and ran past Ray at the finish. Artie O'Conner, my Fordham coach, said he clocked me in 1.43. The world record for the half mile at that time was held by Lon Spurrier at 1.47.5. Lon had run for the University of California and was currently in the Air Force. Lon and I were to compete in the 800-meter final in the 1956 Melbourne Olympics. He finished in fifth place.

Lon and I remained good friends over the years. I once said to Lon, "We ran against one another over a dozen times. I never saw you once. You broke the world record in the half mile running a fast race all the way. Why didn't you ever run a similar race against me?" He said, "I was always afraid if I did that, you would be pulled along and beat me at the finish and take away my world record." He also said that he thought that in every one of those past races, he would be pulled along and beat me at the finish.

CHAPTER 8

On My Own, a Breakthrough in Speed

After I graduated from Fordham, I was on my own. But I knew what to do and each day I tried to improve, to work a little harder, and to become a little faster. One of the things that helped me was when I was in Germany on a trip when I was out of college. There was a fellow named Rudolph Harbig who had held the world record in the 800 meters, but he had been killed in World War II. I went to his house to visit, and his family showed me his diary. He had developed a workout to improve his speed where he ran downhill in a sprint. He said to find a 100-meter downhill and to run it very carefully for the first several months so you wouldn't get injured. When you run downhill, you can put your feet out faster because your body is leaning forward so when you get onto the flat, you can go faster. Arnie Sowell had been beating me for a couple of years and had even run in a West Point meet and won the 100-yard dash in 9.6. I couldn't even break 10 seconds. Eventually before the Olympics, I was running a sprint race in Europe with Ira Murchison who was co-holder of the world record at 9.3, and he only beat me by a hair. So my speed had improved tremendously.

Arnie Sowell was a terrific runner and was my "Chariots of Fire" competitor. I gave him great credit for going out fast to win the Olympics. He felt he could run us into the ground, as he had done in AAU Nationals in Colorado the year earlier. In the Olympics, he started his sprint too early and ran out of gas. I made a mistake and went with him and started to tie up and as I passed Arnie, Derek Johnson shot through between us.

I was so fortunate to regroup and catch Derek at the tape.

CHAPTER 9

"Fastest Man in the World"

In 1956 I ran the 400 at Modesto, California. I felt I had run a poor race and I decided I would run a hard work out of 3x220 yards flat out with a fast jog of 220 yards in between. Dave Sime, who the night before had broken the world record in the 100 and the world record in the 220, asked me if he could take the workout with me. I was surprised but I said certainly. Dave won the first 220, but in the second 220, I passed him with 10 yards to the finish. As I passed him, his leg started to cramp. I told him to stop his workout. His body was warning him that if he continued the next 220, he might pull a muscle. He said he was fine and said, "I guarantee you I will beat you in the third 220." I said, "Dave, you are crazy to continue to run. Anyway, there is no way you are going to beat me in the third 220." We hit our mark on the track and he took off like a shot. As I passed him with 20 yards to go, he again cramped and fell to the ground. He had torn his leg muscle. He told me not to tell anyone. Why was he so insistent? The next week were the National Collegiate Championships and when the starter fired his gun, Dave fell out of his starting block. He was never the same after that. He did come back four years later to run second to Arman Harry of Germany in the 100 meters in the 1960 Olympics. Now you know the rest of the story.

Here was the greatest sprinter of all time, destroyed by his own bad judgment. I felt sorry for him, but for a bright guy from Duke University, he wasn't very smart.

Running requires pushing yourself to new levels. Your body often tells you when to ease off. It is a fine line when you push yourself to surpass that fine line.

When you feel great, that is when you can test yourself. In one practice session, I ran six in and out half miles all under two minutes. Each one harder than the last. It was the hardest workout I had ever done. I could barely stand at the end, but I knew I had extended myself to a new level. The next day I was still exhausted, but two days later I was ready to go again.

Even the Pope Gets into My Story

I had gone to Florence, Italy, to run 800 meters in an Italian track meet. I was running against two good Italian 800-meter men. The meet promoter said if I would run under 1.48, he thought one of those two runners would have a chance to break the Italian record. The Pope had agreed that if I did the sub 1.48 time, he would give me a private audience. I thought that would be wonderful. I told the promoter that to assure that time, I would need the help of a pace-setter. He said they didn't have a runner good enough to help me achieve the time I needed. I said, "Okay, have one of the two runners set the pace, and I would try to then pull the second runner with me for their Italian record." He agreed and said one of those two would run the first lap in 51 seconds and then last as long as possible.

What happened was that neither one of the two went out as a pacesetter, and while I was waiting for the pacesetter to run out in 51 seconds for the first 400, I was lagging back and I heard the 400 time of 56. Now I realized what had happened and saw my private audience with the Pope disappearing. I took off like a shot and ended up winning the race in 1.47. The two Italian runners got left in the dust and broke no Italian record that day. Since I did run under 1.48, I felt I deserved the private audience with the Pope. Instead he welshed on his promise.

I did not see the Pope, nor did I want to see a Pope who would not insist on honoring his commitment. Probably the Pope never heard of the promoter and my agreement, nor of me.

When we ran in a town, the promoter wanted us to try to break the world record. Some of these towns had poor tracks and there was no chance to run an exceptional time, but the promoter wanted you to try anyway. I understood that, but it was essential to save yourself once in a while. When you find yourself competing against a top runner, on a good track you wanted to perform your best.

Going to L.A. for the Olympic Trials

I went out to Los Angeles with Bob Rittenburg. Bob had been a great hurdler at Harvard. We had trained together at Fort Dix. Both of us hoped to make the Olympic Team. I was going to try and run the 400 meters and the 800 meters. Bob was trying to make the team in the 400 hurdles.

I was at a luncheon one day while we were training for the Olympic Trials when a fellow was telling how he had an auto that was driving him crazy. Every time he stopped the car, he had to turn off the motor and use the starter to get it going. The car was a lemon. The battery went down in no time. He said if someone would give him a $1.00 and get him off the owner's paper, he would take it. I handed him $1.00 and took over ownership of the car.

In cleaning the car, I found $1.65 under the front seats. Bob and I had to get several battery charges. We discovered that if we parked on a hill, we could get it going the next day. One morning we were parked on a rather steep hill and there was another car right in front of us. Bob said he had seen a car repair shop about a block away and walked down to it. He said he told the owner of the shop of our predicament and as we were in our Army uniforms, the shop owner came up and towed the car to his shop and fixed the problem with the starter. Bob said he might have promised the guy to come back to work there after he got out of the service, but he wasn't sure.

We then had a car that we operated for a number of weeks before the Olympic Trials.

Now with a car that worked and the help of one of my Fordham roommates, Carl Candel, I got a date with Judy Lewis. She was the daughter of Loretta Young and Clark Gable. Later I invited Judy and her mother to the Coliseum Relays. I was inspired that night and broke the world record for the half mile in 1.46. Unfortunately Judy had to go back to NYC to be in the soap opera, "General Hospital."

I was invited to be on the *Ed Sullivan Show*. I was named with Carol Lawrence to be Mr. and Mrs. Heart in the Heart Drive, and I was named King with the Queen of Hearts with Miss Rheingold.

When we visited one movie studio, Jayne Mansfield asked me for my autograph. She handed me a picture that had been in a magazine along with a pen. I looked around for a place to hold the photo, and she took it and held it on her famous chest. Being a runner was far better than I imagined!

Jack Kelly and Tom were asked to model
the 1956 Olympic clothes.

I was asked to model the Olympic outfits with Jack Kelly. We were friends and after that he asked me if I would go on a date with his sister, Grace Kelly, of movie fame.

At that time she was considered the best-looking girl in the movies. I said sure and he set me up and I picked her up at the Barbizon Plaza. We had a nice time and I asked her for another date. She said she was going to Monaco the next week, and the next thing I knew was she was getting engaged to Prince Rainier. The rest was history—too bad.

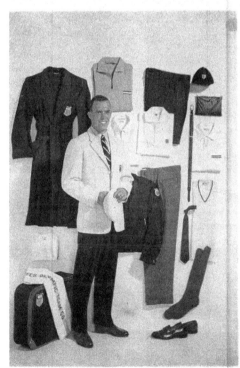

SPORTING LOOK

WELL OUTFITTED FOR MELBOURNE

The best-dressed team we've ever sent to an Olympiad wears uniforms donated by American manufacturers

PHOTOGRAPHS BY RICHARD MEEK

WHEN America's 440-member Olympic team—including the athletes, coaches and officials—parades into the stadium at Melbourne for next Thursday's opening day ceremonies, they will be uniformly dressed in eggshell worsted blazers piped in blue, gold Olympic buttons glinting in the Australian sun, the U.S. Olympic shield ablaze on pockets and on cream-colored berets. The men will be wearing trousers of navy worsted; the women, skirts to match. And after opening day, all through the Games, the Americans down under, whether on the field or at leisure, will be uniformly clothed in a manner that will do the U.S. proud. For the first time our athletes, coaches and officials have been completely outfitted—from underwear out—with travel, parade and leisure uniforms, all given to the Olympic Supplies Committee by the textile and clothing manufacturers of the U.S., with the coordinating assistance of the Wool Bureau. For H. Jamison Swarts and his supplies committee, this solved a $127,000 problem. The only headaches left were minor ones—such as having a custom uniform tailored for Weight Lifter Paul Anderson of Toccoa, Ga., whose neck is 23½ inches and chest is 55 inches. Even with Anderson included, the average Olympian is only slightly larger than the average young American—42-inch-long suits for the men; size 14 for the girls. In addition to the uniforms, a variety of other items has been given to the athletes. The West German firm of Puma-Dassler gave 190 pairs of track shoes. Jantzen and Sacony furnished the girls with swimsuits and track uniforms, Kleinert with swim caps. Atlantic Products gave luggage and Martex 125 dozen towels. And Beech-Nut gave the team a two weeks' supply of chewing gum.

MEN'S OFFICIAL OLYMPIC UNIFORM

Tom Courtney, who will run the 800 meters for the U.S., wears his official parade uniform. Behind him are more of his 26 different items of apparel: bathrobe, pajamas, sports and dress shirts, raincoat, sweater, cap, slacks, travel jacket, luggage and towel. Most of the actual participating gear—such as Courtney's track uniform—was purchased by the Olympic Supplies Committee at cost.

Well Outfitted for Melbourne

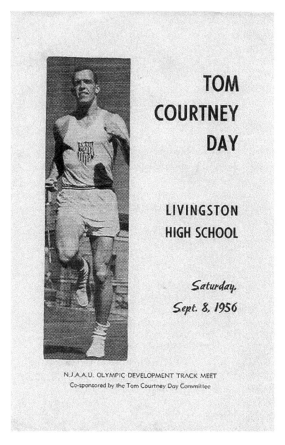

TOM
COURTNEY
DAY

LIVINGSTON
HIGH SCHOOL

Saturday,
Sept. 8, 1956

N.J.A.A.U. OLYMPIC DEVELOPMENT TRACK MEET
Co-sponsored by the Tom Courtney Day Committee

Livinvston was proud of its Olympian

Tom Courtney Day 1956

After the Trials and making the team, I didn't know what to do with the car. Lon Spurrier, my teammate, told me he knew where I could park it until I came back in the fall. When I got back Lon and I took a cab out to the field where we had left it. The cab gave me a charge and it started. I saw one of the tires was a little flat and I knocked off the hub cap. The car was full of black widow spiders. I chased them away and got in to drive the car. Lon meanwhile had taken out a coat hanger, straightened it out, and sitting at the far right window, ran the coat hanger up behind the seat and said, "Tom, there's a black widow on your neck." I smashed the supposed spider with a fast hard blow. I had a big cut in my neck and did not think Lon's sense of humor was funny. Going out to the field, I had seen a sign at an auto shop saying, "We buy any auto that drives into our lot." Realizing the last thing I needed was an actual black widow bite, I pulled into the lot. The owner offered me one hundred dollars, which I accepted, along with a ride into town. As we left him, I mentioned that we had seen some spiders in the car. He said, "Forget it. That field was full of black widows. I'll take care of them."

Hollywood and Celebrities

John Wayne was on the set for the movie, *The Conquerer*. Artie O'Conner, our coach, took us to the set as arranged by his cousin, Melvin Leroy. Leroy was a major movie director at that time. We overheard John Wayne. He said, "Who are those people?"

Our guide said we were the two-mile relay team from Fordham University that broke the world record last night. Wayne said, "I don't care who they are. Get them the hell out of here." The guide said they were invited by Melvin Leroy. At that John Wayne came right over to us and said what a great honor it was to meet us. "Let me take you around."

I went to a swim party at Gregory Peck's house. He wasn't there, but his wife gave me one of his swimsuits. She said he wouldn't need it at her house anymore. I was quite impressed that Peck had a 32-inch waist.

Howard Cosell saw me in Jamaica years later, after the Olympics. He introduced me to his wife and described my Olympic 800-meter race to her. He knew my time for the race 1.47. Quite an amazing memory. While I was running, he invited me on his TV show. He wanted to know my position on the battle that was taking place between the AAU and the NCAA. I said I wasn't going to get involved in that debate. He then said, "Tom, strictly off the record, what is your position?" I confided in him. Then he opened up his program saying, "Tom Courtney has just told me his position on the AAU and NCAA argument and Tom felt the AAU was wrong for the following reasons." I was floored by what Howard did. I got up and said, "Howard, you told me what I said was totally off the record," and I walked off the show.

Olympic Trials

I had qualified in the 800 meters for the US Olympic Trials at the All-Service Championships. To qualify for the 400 meters, I ran the 400 in the National AAU Championships. I was in the fifth lane, and Charlie Jenkins was in the fourth lane. I knew that if I stayed with Charlie, I would be in good shape. Off the last turn, I went around Jenkins and won by six meters in a new AAU and American record of 45 seconds.

The next week in the US Olympic Trials, I decided to run both the 800 meters and the 400 meters. Unlike today's ten-day trials, these were a two-day affair. I ran my 800 qualifier on Friday and won my heat. On Saturday I ran the 800-meter final and won in a new American record of 1.46 seconds, beating my archrival, Arnie Sowell. Lon Spurrier was third; Mal Whitfield was a distant fifth. The very next event was the 400-meter heats. I went out to set up my starting blocks. I was still totally exhausted from the 800-meter race, and when I got down in my blocks, my head was pounding and I started to sway dizzily. I walked over to the starter and withdrew.

Charlie Jenkins won the 400 meters in the 1956 Olympics. The 400 heats, semis, and final were on days after my 800-meter victory. At the Olympics, unlike at the two days for the trials, the events were run over ten days. I would have had no problem in running both the 800 meters and the 400 meters. I had pleaded with Head Olympic

Coach Jim Kelly to let me run on the 1600-meter relay team. Kelly told me that J. W. Mashburn from Oklahoma University had been the fourth man in the 1952 Olympics, but Charlie Moore, the 400-meter hurdle champion from Cornell, had taken his place on the relay team. Kelly said he could not let a runner go to two Olympics and not run.

A week before the Olympic Games in a town called Bendigo, Australia, Coach Kelly told the four 400-meter men that he was having them run against me and that if any one of them beat me, I would not be put on the relay team. This foursome included Charles Jenkins (who won the Olympic 400 meters), Lou Jones (who currently held the world 400-meter record), Jimmy Lea (who held the world 440-yard record), and J. W. Mashburn. I won the race and thought I had made the relay team. I was overjoyed, but Coach Kelly said that only if I had been beaten, I would not be on the relay team. He still felt strongly that he had to let Mashburn run.

In the end Kelly was good to his pledge. He substituted me for Jimmy Lea, who had not run his best in the Olympic 400. In the heats I ran the third leg. But in the final Kelly put me in as the anchor. Our team won by 15 yards.

Why was trying to win the 800 meters, the 400 meters, and the relay so important to me?

There was a poem by Sterling B. Sill taped to our refrigerator as we grew up. It read. "The average man's complacent when he has done his best to score, but the champion does his best, and then he does a little more." I guess I saw triple in that quote.

CHAPTER 13

Louis Zamperini—Unbroken

I used to practice at the University of Southern California's track. Southern Cal had many track men competing in the Olympic Trials. They also had many past Olympians. One was a 5,000-meter freshman who ran fifth in the 1936 Olympics in Germany. He didn't win but finished with such a tremendous finishing kick, that Hitler had him visit to congratulate him. It was Louis Zamperini. He told Hitler he intended to win the 1500 meters in 1940. Those games were cancelled due to World War 11, and Zamperini was in a Japanese prison camp.

At my Olympic Trials, he came down to the Coliseum Track to talk to me after my semifinals and told me to just stay with the pack in the finals and outsprint the others off the final turn. I did just that in the finals. Again Zamperini came to see me after the finish. He seemed pleased that I had used his advice. He wished me luck at the Olympics and said he knew I would win in Melbourne.

I did not know of his unbelievable story during the war until years later when I read Laura Hildebrand's best-seller, *Unbroken*. Many years later he came to give a talk at a church in Naples, Florida. I took my wife, Posy, and brother, Jim, to hear him speak. We tried to see him, but there was such a huge crowd that the organizers only allowed past World War II veterans into the main hall. His talk was inspirational, but we did not get to see him. He died shortly after that.

CHAPTER 14

Our Trip to Melbourne

The Olympic Trials were held at the Los Angeles Coliseum in the beginning of July 1956. The Olympic Games were to be held in Melbourne, Australia, in November. For four months we were on our own. I went back to Boston training on my own. I trained very hard, one day running eight in and out 800 meters for my workout. On the other hand, Jimmy Lea, one of the 400-meter runners, came back four months later having gained twenty-five pounds, and he never regained his keen condition.

The seasons were reversed in Australia and their summer began in December. The Olympic Games were held in November and should have been held in December because it was still cold and windy in Melbourne.

I flew from Boston to Los Angeles in October. We had three practice meets before we left for Australia. In these meets I ran against Arnie Sowell and Lon Spurrier, the two other 800-meter men. We also ran a 4x400 relay against the four men who had qualified for the relay team. Our team included Glen Davis, the top 400-meter hurdles runner. We beat the qualified relay team every time. I was in second place each time on the anchor leg, but we won all three races.

I used the 800 races to try to convince Arnie Sowell to run a fast pace in the Olympic final. Arnie had been my motivation. At the University of Pittsburgh, he had come along as a freshman and beaten me in my junior year at Fordham in the 1C4A Championships. For the next several years, he had my number. With my newly acquired speed, I had beaten him in the Olympic Trials. The year before in the AAU Championships in Colorado, Arnie had run with a very fast pace and won with an American record. I knew he felt that was his best race and would likely use that strategy in the Olympic final. I felt that fast pace would help me and would give me my best chance.

Our trip from Los Angeles took us to Hawaii, where we spent two days. We all posed separately with Miss Hawaii in front of the Royal Hawaiian Hotel. Next we flew to the Fiji Islands, then on to Canton Island for refueling. We were in an Air Force plane and it was just the men's track team. The water was beautiful so we stripped down and went for a swim in the ocean. It was fairly shallow so forty or fifty of us had to go out quite a ways. When we got out deep enough for our swim, a giant 14- or 15-foot shark came between us and the land. The fact that we had no bathing suits made us all the more nervous. We debated what to do, and hoped some help would arrive, but it did not. Finally after coming up with no plan, we broke into a mass run for the beach, waving one hand at the shark and the other protecting our family jewels.

On the way to Melbourne Australia Olympics.
Stayed at the Royal Hawaii Hotel.

Photo with Miss Hawaii.

Our next stop was Melbourne, Australia, and we were happy to arrive. I roomed with Jack Davis, the favorite in the 110-meter hurdles. Jack lost in the final to Lee Calhoun and went into shock. He never said a word to me or anyone else for the next two weeks. It was quite unnerving, to say the least.

CHAPTER 15

To Win the Ultimate Gold

The 1956 Olympic 800 Had to Be Won Twice

Half-milers get very old in four years. Rarely do you get a second chance to win the Olympics. Until you compete, you never realize how fortunate you are to be at your best the year of the Olympics, the month of the Olympics, the day of your event. A string of trials causes the tension to build up to a high tempo. In the heats, trials and semifinals you have to be ready, but you have to be perfect in the Finals.

If you wake up that morning with a cold or even a stomachache, it's all over. It is not like the national championships which take place every year, if you lose, you can always come back next year to redeem yourself.

When I first started running, my father wanted to discuss my tactics for the State High School Championships. I got so nervous, I left the room and got sick. Over the years, that feeling disappeared. With time and confidence, I became very relaxed. Before the Metropolitan Championships that year, I went into the locker room to stretch out a half-hour before race time and fell asleep. My brother Brian rushed in, shook me, and said "What the heck are you doing? They are on the starting line for the Finals!"

The day of the Olympic final had arrived. We were down in Melbourne, Australia, in 1956. We were running the 800 meters. This was the race I had dreamed about for years. An Olympic title is more important than even a world record. Maybe it is because of the competition and that you have to beat the best of the world on that day. Maybe it is because you realize it is the only time you will run in the Olympics.

As I stepped on the track, my legs went rubbery. I found that I could not stand up and I sagged to the grass. I saw the hundred thousand people in the stands, and thought, is it possible that I am so nervous that I won't be able to run today?

The excitement was so strenuous that I started to panic. Then it occurred to me that I was going to look silly out there on the grass as they started the Finals of the 800 meters. I guess the humor of the situation overcame the nervousness, I was able to recover, get up, and jog to the starting line. As I approached the starting line, I saw my teammate and arch rival, Arnie Sowell. When the great Norwegian Audun Boysen had come over to the United States the year before and was beaten by Arnie Sowell in the indoor national champion-ships, the paper gave headlines to his quote, "Take care of Sowell, he is your next Olympic Champion." Most experts picked Arnie to be the next Olympic Champion.

Arnie had come along as an unknown in my junior year at Fordham. I was undefeated that year and the odds-on favorite in the Inter-Collegiate 880-yard race. When this young, slender speedster from Pittsburgh sped by me after the first lap. I thought, I better pass him right now, but I knew I could wait and outkick him off the final turn and that would be much more exciting. There was no excitement for me that day. I started my kick down the final straight-away. I pulled within inches, but slowly and to my chagrin, Sowell took those long strides, made them a little longer, and beat me to the tape. I was unable to catch him for several years. But in trying to catch Arnie, I trained so hard and got into such good condition that I was ready to race against him and the rest of the world that day. My other teammate and great friend, Lon Spurrier, was also in the

Finals. Lon held the world's record of the half-mile. Word had gotten around that Lon had the flu earlier in the week, but I knew Lon well and knew he was going to be up there at the finish, even if he had a broken leg. Audun Boyson, the great Champion from Norway, held most of the 1,000-meter records in Europe. He had come over to the United States for the indoor season and with the exception of that one defeat to Sowell, he won all the indoor races. Today he loomed larger than he looked indoors. England's Derek Johnson was someone I secretly feared. We had raced in England and I had a 15-yard lead going into the last turn, but at the tape he missed beating me by inches. The others in the Final were Mike Farrel of England. Leva of Belgium and Bill Butchard of Australia. They were good and all confident of victory, but I considered them as unknown potential threats.

The field might very well have included two of the other top runners in the world: Jim Bailey of Australia and Gunnar Nielsen of Denmark. Both had broken four minutes for the mile and were exceptionally strong 800-meter men. Nielsen had won the European games in the 800 that year, and Bailey was the British Empire 800 Champion. To this day I believe they were not in the race because of a strategic ploy by Olympic coach Bob Giegengack, the erudite coach from Yale University. During the week of the heats, Bob took me to a practice track for a workout. The track had been under a terrific downpour and was very heavy. The day was extremely cold at 40 degrees and the wind was ripping. I debated whether or not even to run, but Gieg insisted I needed a workout for pace. Just as I was about to run-through the practice 800-meters, Bob pulled me aside and said to me: "Tom, down at the end of the track I saw Jim Bailey and Gunnar Neilsen sitting in a car watching your workout. Run a sub 1.50 half on this track today and those two guys will decide to run the 1500 meters."

With a big smile, trying to make it look easy and relaxed, I went as hard as I possibly could that day and came in at 1:49. Geigengack claimed it was the equivalent of at least a 1:46 another day. Two days later, I virtually danced from the dining room to my dorm when

I heard that Bailey and Nelson had both dropped out of the 800 meters and decided to run the 1500 meters.

The other man I half expected to see turn up was Mal Whitfield. Mal was a legend when I started running, He had held eleven different world records and had won the 1948 and 1952 Olympics. The year before the 1956 Olympics, he still looked like the man to beat, having made the Pan-American Team. One thing I had learned while I was running was that most runners duplicated what they considered their finest race when the pressure is really on. Mal did exactly that in the U.S. trials for Melbourne. In the Olympics in Finland in 1952, he had run a record-breaking 1:49 winning the 800 meters. He had done it by accelerating on the back stretch, building a substantial lead, and then holding off the opposition on the final straightaway. It was also fascinating that Mal Whitfield's time, although he took 5th in the race, was 1.49.

Remembering this lesson, I worked to set Arnie Sowell up to lead the pace in the Olympic Final. I knew that if the pace was very fast, I would have an advantage, because I always had a strong finish. I did not want it to be a race where, due to a slow pace, I could get boxed or have someone shoot out at a certain point and steal it. It had to be a race where we all ran to our ultimate with the results resting upon the man who was able to hit the tape first. Arnie Sowell had set an American record from the front in the Denver National Championships the year before. We had run heats and passed out because of the high altitude. In the finals, everyone but Sowell assumed that it would be wise to take it easy the first quarter mile and then blast the last quarter.

Sowell did not think so. He went out fast, established a 40-yard lead, and although we closed it to a yard, none of us could catch him at the tape. We all passed out after the finals. But it had little effect on our running.

As the American team prepared for the Olympics earlier in the month, I ran against Arnie three times. I knew he felt he could beat me with a fast pace, but he did not want to show his hand. Each time he ran a slow pace. Each time I waited behind him and outsprinted him off the last turn. I felt this would convince him to run back to his Denver race the day of the final competition in Melbourne. This strategy caused a more exciting race than I had ever anticipated.

The gun sounded. I led until the first turn, but Sowell took right over, and we followed one another in that order until we went into the last turn. The first lap was blisteringly fast: .51. At this pace, I knew we would not have more than a 60- or 70-yard finishing kick. But all of a sudden, with at least 140 yards to go, Sowell started his final sprint. I knew it was too early, and he would die before the finish. At least I thought it was too early. If I went with him, I would not be able to finish. Yet I just could not run the risk that Sowell could somehow sprint the rest of the way. What if Sowell had a super Olympic effort and stole the race. I went after him with about 120 yards to the tape. I caught Arnie on the turn and slowly passed him. I was clear, but wanted to get to firmer ground away from the chewed-up inside lane. I moved out into the third lane. Suddenly Derek Johnson—where did he come from? —spurted through the hole between Sowell and me with just 50 yards to go. As Derek went by, I had started to tie up. The sprint was over for me, my legs were getting rubbery, my head was bobbling, and my body stiffening. I was finished. Once before after I had lost a race by dying in the final stretch, I thought to myself, if I had really been able to conquer the pain barrier, physically I might have been able to fight it out to the tape. My thoughts were that maybe I could recover. But not with so little to go. And not when you are being outsprinted. But I looked at the tape with just 40 yards to go and realized this was the only chance I would ever have to win the Olympics. I did not want to finish thinking I might have put a little more into it. So I put everything I had into it. I leaned as far forward as I could and threw my arms out ahead of me. Step by step somehow, I started to move again. Somehow I pulled up even with Johnson with almost no yards to go. There was the line. I lunged. I won by less than one-tenth of a second. It was a new Olympic record: 1:47.7. The first five runners all broke the old Olympic record. Sowell had run us into a state of exhaustion, including himself.

Before the games, I often asked myself how it would feel to win. I couldn't answer that, but I knew how it would feel if I lost. People often wonder what runners think about during a race. Throughout this race, I kept asking myself that question. Actually, at the finish I did not even know I had won. Derek Johnson came over to congratulate me and said I had nicked him at the tape. I tried to thank Derek, but I was on my feet and staggering. I had to get off the track because I was starting to pass out. With the help of some teammates, I reached the locker room and collapsed. The strange thing was that I was not unconscious. Physically, I was unable to move. I was so totally exhausted. I was in a state of total oxygen deficit. It was a new kind agony for me. I had never run myself into such a state. My head was exploding, my stomach ripping, and even the tips of my fingers ached. The only thing I could think was, "If I live, I will never run again!" People around me thought I was unconscious, but I was not. They had to hold up the awards ceremony for over an hour.

Coming around the last turn at the 800 meter
final at Olympics Nov. 26, 1956
L to R Mike Farrell - Great Britain
Audun Boysen - Norway
Lon Spurrier - USA
Tom Courtney - USA
Derek Johnson - Great Britain
Arnie Sowell - USA
Winner Tom Courtney 1.47.7 New Olympic Record
2nd Derek Johnson
3rd Audun Boysen

Finish of 800 meters

Olympic 4x400 Relay Winners

When they played the National Anthem, I had already forgotten the pain and all I could think of was how thankful I was that the year was right, the day was right, and I was ready. I thought to myself. I've wondered how it would feel to win the Olympics. The next day I ran on the 4x400 relay team. We won the final several days later. Coach Kelly had me run the anchor leg to win the gold—that was a great thrill. The team included first leg Lou Jones, second leg J.W. Mashburn, third leg Charlie Jenkins, and anchor Tom Courtney.

After the Olympics

I was so enthusiastic about the Australian people because they were very open and friendly in those days, and they still are like that. Their enthusiasm impressed me tremendously. I didn't even go to the opening ceremonies because I was there to try to win the 800 meters and I didn't want to stay up and to march around the field. We were amateurs, and I was hopeful that it would work out well for the Australians and their hosting of the Olympics, but I was very focused as everything I did for those two weeks was in preparation for my event. I did not go to the closing ceremonies as they sent a group of us up to Sydney where we ran a series of races of the United Stated versus the British Empire. In Sydney, we broke the world record in the mile relay and the two-mile relay.

Fordham Parade

When I got back to the States, I appeared on the *Ed Sullivan Show*. There was a big party at Leone's Restaurant, and a wonderful parade down Fordham Road. That was a lovely time and I was in a convertible with my coach, Artie O'Conner. I was very lucky to have him as my coach. He was very motivational for me. As we went along, he took my losses much harder than I did. He was a dedicated, wonderful man. He loved Fordham and it helped me to love Fordham. He told me when I went out to California to run in the Olympic Trials. "Now, Tom, three guys get to go to the Olympics in each event, so if Arnie beats you, that's okay. You can get second." This was my coach who was a great motivator. So when I went to the National AAU Championships and won the 400 meters, he called me and said, "I didn't realize you were that fast. Go for it!"

William Brucker, Secretary of the Army, greets Olympians.

L to R Ira Murchinson, John Bennett, Secretary
Brucker, Tom Courtney, Lou Jones

Celebrity Awards Night 1956

Don Budge - tennis, Charlie Connerly - Giants, Keith
Morris - Sports Illustrated, Carol Fagarera - golf champion,
Althea Gibson golf and tennis Champion, Florence
Chadwick - swam the English Channel, Buster Crabbe -
swimmer and movie star, Tom Courtney- Track and Field.

After the Olympics, I continued to run in the indoor track
meets. I broke the world indoor record for 600 yards. Outdoors I
won the AAU Championship's and was offered a trip to Switzerland,
Germany, France, England, Scotland, and Ireland. Later that year I
went on a trip to Africa with Artie O'Conner, my former Fordham
coach. I was sick as a dog and could hardly swallow. I was going to
cancel the trip, but I knew it was Coach O'Conner's only trip he had
ever won, so I went. When we got to South Africa, my first meet was
in Port Elizabeth at night on a grass track. I lost badly. But two weeks
later in Johannesburg, I raced Mal Spence, an Olympian in the 400,

and David Lee in the 800. I broke the South African record in both races and Artie O'Conner was happy—and so was I.

Second Annual

UNIVERSITY OF HOUSTON
Invitational

Tom Courtney
Breaks World Record

MEET OF CHAMPIONS

25c

Public School Stadium
Houston, Texas

June 8, 1957
6:45 P.M.

1956 Tom setting new world record at the Coliseum Relays

Charlie Jenkins was second on outside.

Excerpts from Fordham Digest

Tom Courtney's winning of the 800-meter race at Melbourne in the Olympics made him the first gold medal Olympic winner in the history of Fordham. Artie O'Conner, coach of track, asserts that "Tom is the greatest runner Fordham has ever had." There are those on the campus who state that Tom's achievement was the greatest athletic achievement ever accomplished by a Fordham athlete.

Prior to the race, Fr. Stephen O'Beirne celebrated a special Mass for Tom and the success of his Olympic endeavors in the University church Wednesday, November 21, 1956, as a "Mass of Petition for his efforts in the Olympics." Members of the present track team, their coach, and the student body were present at the Mass. Hearing of this Mass by letter from Fr. O'Beirne, Tom Courtney replies as follows before his championship race:

> Dear Father O'Beirne,
>
> I just received your letter and I want you to know how much I appreciate the Mass and all the prayers. I know that I can't receive better assistance than the help of the Lord. I have been both training hard and praying myself and I hope I am able to do my best when the final gun is fired. With the help of everyone up at school I'm feeling quite confident these days. I must admit I'm quite nervous at this point and chances are that when you receive this letter you will know how the 800 meters was run.
>
> Whatever the outcome, I want you to give my sincere thanks to all the Priests and others at Fordham who were good enough to remember me.

Fordham has been very good to me. I received a fine education, Artie was a great coach, and one just can't measure the value of one's friends.

Thank you again.

Sincerely,
Tom Courtney

The University will honor Tom at a special ceremony upon his return to the United States. He will be Guest of Honor at the Christmas Party of The Spike Shoe Club the evening of Saturday, December 8, from four to seven. There will be a parade from the Concourse to Fordham gym on Wednesday morning, December 12, 1956, after the first period. The University will award Tom a trophy commemorating his Olympic victory and the fact that he is Fordham's *First Gold Medal winner* in history. The undergraduate ceremonies will be followed by a Sportswriters and Broadcasters Luncheon in his honor at Leone's Restaurant. Arrangements for Tom Courtney Day are under the direction of Fr. Yanitelli, assisted by Fr. Healy and Bob O'Conner of the Alumni Office and the track coach, Artie O'Conner.

CHAPTER 17

Emil Zatopek—Sweeping Streets

On one of my European trips, I ran in Prague, Czechoslovakia. I met Olga Fikotova, the European discus Olympic champion. She introduced me to Emil Zatopek and his wife, Dana. Zatopek was the king of the running world, winning the 10,000 meters, the 5,000 meters, and the Marathon in the 1952 Olympics in Helsinki. His wife, Dana, also won the javelin in the same Olympics.

He was a good Czech soldier and praised by his Communist paymasters. Unfortunately his coach, Jan Haluza, was falsely accused of being a spy and sent to prison and was violently treated. Zatopek tried to defend his former coach and ended losing his position of captain of the tank corps, to sweeping streets in Prague. He was an enthusiastic man who tried to help everyone, even his competitors. At dinner one night, he asked me if I was in the army. I said yes. He said what is your rank? I said private. He didn't believe me. He said when he won three gold medals in the Olympics in 1952, they made him a captain. He said after I won the two gold medals in 1956, you would think they would at least have made me a lieutenant.

When Harold Connolly (who had won the hammer throw at the 1956 Olympics) met Olga Fikotova at the Melbourne Olympics, they fell in love. Harold went over to Czechoslovakia in 1957 to marry Olga. The Communists refused to allow Harold into the country. So he waited at the border. With Zatopek's help, the president allowed the wedding.

CHAPTER 18

The Boston Army Base 1956

When I came back to the Boston Army Base from the Olympics, the commanding officer called me in to congratulate me. He said since I am now in the Army, I would have to give up my running. I said, "Colonel Hull in Washington told me I should run in all the major meets representing the Army." He said that those days were over.

I left his office and called Colonel Hull. I had also developed a good relationship with a colonel at the Boston Army Base. He was retiring after thirty years of service and had just sold his car to me, which I then sold to my brother, Brian. He worked in the Communication office. When he saw the message from Colonel Hull to the Boston commander, he ran over and told me what it said. "We are proud of our two-gold-medal Olympian Tom Courtney. We want him to represent the Army in all the major meets. Give him whatever time he needs to train to perform at his best."

Shortly after that, the commanding officer called me back to his office. He said he had reconsidered things and that I should run in all the major meets representing the Army. He asked me to give him a schedule of the time I needed for training.

I had already prepared a schedule and handed it to him. From 9 to 12 o'clock, I needed to do distance training on the banks of the Charles River. From 1 to 4 in the afternoon, I needed to do sprint training at the Harvard Track. He blanched as he looked at my schedule and signed his name approving it. He thanked me and I left with his approved schedule.

There was one final review before I went to the Harvard Business School. A new commanding officer came to the Boston Army Base. He had us all line up to meet him. As he came to me, he asked what the insignia I was wearing was. I said it was my basic training insignia. He asked how long I had been in the Army. I said I was getting out the next week. He eyes glazed over and he went on to the next soldier.

CHAPTER 19

Harvard Business School

A fter the Olympics, Jim Kelly, the head coach of the track team, asked me to visit with his foster son, Les Rollins. Les was a dean at the Harvard Business School and had been a runner in his college days at Buena Vista College. When I returned to Boston, I called Dean Rollins and set up a time to visit. He was a very enthusiastic person and we talked for well over an hour. At that point he said, "What makes you think you are good enough to go to the Harvard Business School?" I said, "I'm not going to the Harvard Business School. I am going to go to Law School." He said, "No, you are not. You are going to the Harvard Business School."

The next day he called me at the Boston Army Base and said there were two professors at the school that wanted to have dinner with me. Always looking for a free meal, I went to dinner with them. A few days later, Rollins called me and said he had two students that wanted to buy me dinner. I again agreed. Rollins set up other lunches and dinners and had me meet his fellow dean, Vernon Alden.

Now I had gone up to Boston from Fort Dix with Bob Rittenburg accepting the invitation of the Harvard track coach Bill McCurdy to train and live at the Varsity Club. Bob said he had decided to take the business school exam and that the track coach at Boston English (who was also the English teacher) had agreed to help Bob and me prepare for the exam if we would come over once a week to help his track team. I decided since I wasn't getting any mental educational stimulation, I would do this and agreed to go with Rittenburg. We ended up taking the exam. Unfortunately Bob did not get accepted but I did. I gave a great deal of thought to it, but in the end decided it was a terrific opportunity and I went to the business school. It was a very difficult school.

I requested getting out of the Army a few weeks early and permission was granted to allow me to start school on the opening day.

When I went to the Harvard Business School, I retired from track. Between my two years, I had secured a summer job at Kidder Peabody.

1958 Tom's Harvard Business School photo for the class of 1959.

The US army notified me I was going to have to go back into the Army for summer camp in a reserve unit for eight weeks. I was told that Russia had challenged the USA to a track meet in Moscow, and if I went to the Russian meet, I would be excused from the summer Army camp. All I had to do was to qualify in the 800 meters in the AAU National Championships and I could go on the Russian trip. I had a few weeks to train. I went to the Nationals in California and won the race. We went to Europe and ran a couple of meets and then went to Moscow. I won the 800, and the USA men defeated the Russian team. The Russians also had a women's meet. They promised the meets would be separate. Naturally the Russians combined the men's and women's points and claimed they won the meet. (At that time we were in a cold war climate.) We ended up running in a few more meets in Europe. The last meet was in Athens, Greece, and then I was returning to the United States to resume my second year at the Harvard Business School. A group of us from the men's and women's track team decided to go out to Star Beach that morning. After a swim, I went up on the beach to rest. Unfortunately I fell asleep and got a very bad sunburn. That evening we were running at the 1896 Stadium that hosted the First Modern Olympics. It had long straight aways and extremely narrow turns, and a poor track. I was upset with myself. The swim and severe sunburn had left me in a limp form. I ended up losing my last race. I had been extremely fool-ish thinking I could do these things and still win the race. I deserved a dose of humility and got it. The lesson I learned was that if one wants to continue at a high level, you have to maintain your skills and stay focused on your goals.

On my return, I worked the rest of the summer at Kidder Peabody & Co. in New York City. The senior partner was Albert Gordon.

In my second year, I was offered a job as assistant track coach at Harvard. I said I was too busy. They offered to double that salary. I said no. They offered to triple the salary. I asked how many hours a day. They said two and I took the job.

One of my charges was young Albie Gordon, a quarter miler. After a few meets, Mr. Gordon Sr. talked to me about Albie's goal to break the Harvard quarter mile record. I thought Albie was a good runner, but probably not capable of breaking the Harvard record. Mr. Gordon offered me a bonus if I helped him do it. I said I gave all my boys my best effort. He said he would double the bonus. I said no. He then said he would triple the bonus. I then knew who was paying my assistant track coaching salary.

I did agree to talk to Albie and said I would give him some extra help, but he would probably get to hate me and end up throwing up in the bushes. I told him to think about it over the weekend and then tell me his decision. He came back on Monday and was ready to go. A few days later he was throwing up in the bushes. A few weeks later at the Harvard Yale meet in New Haven, he beat a very good Yale runner named Jim Stack and broke the Harvard record.

Later I went to work at Kidder Peabody under the senior partner, Mr. Albert Gordon. At an opportune time, I told Mr. Gordon how I was enjoying working at the firm, but also he had never given me the bonus for helping his son break the Harvard quarter mile record. Mr. Gordon said he would take care of it. But he never did.

Albert Gordon loved his family, Harvard, and track. At age 82, he set a world senior's record for two miles of sixteen minutes and 12 seconds. He would say, "Tom, we are going up to Fishers Island this weekend." I would say, "Yes, sir." He also brought his daughter, Mary, with us. We would go to the dances. A few weeks later, he said, "Tom, we are going up to Fishers Island for the weekend." I asked if I could bring a friend. He said, "What is his name?" I said, "Posy."

Tom Courtney and Posy L'Hommedieu visiting Fishers
Island with Albie Gordon and his wife Valer.

Posy L'Hommedieu and I had met in Oyster Bay at young Albie Gordon's and Valer Clark's weekend engagement party. Posy had gone to Paris on the Hollins Abroad Program. Posy and Valer were good friends. At the end of the weekend, I offered to drive Posy and her twin sister, Abby, back to New York. Posy had told Abby that since she liked Tom to sit in the front with him. Abby said, "No, Tom likes you. You get in the front seat." Lynn Santee, another girl I was driving into town, started to get in the front. I said I had promised Posy the ride provided she would sit next to me in the front seat. That was the beginning of a fairytale romance for me. I fell in love with her, and after two years, we were married in Lancaster, Pennsylvania. We went to the Bahamas on our honeymoon and returned to Jacksonville, Florida, where I had taken a new position as vice president of investments for Peninsular Life Insurance Company.

Life was good! We had six wonderful years in Jacksonville. We started to raise our family of three wonderful boys, Tom Jr. and Peter. Then I took a new job in New York City with MacKay Shields. We lived in Connecticut, where Frank was born. Later Posy would say she had 19 feet of children: Tom Jr., 6'4", Peter, 6'6", and Frank, 6'2".

Posy and our first son, Tom jr.

CHAPTER 20

Sand in an Airplane Gas Tank
and a Price on My Head

The first day I arrived at Peninsular Insurance Co. in 1962, Larry Lee, the chairman, said he wanted me to look at an investment deal from the investment firm Hayden Stone. It was something similar to what I had worked on up in NYC. After reviewing it, I told Larry why I wouldn't recommend it. He went back to his office and called Claude Kirk, and told him he was dropping out of the deal. Kirk said Larry had agreed to do it. Larry said he had to use the first advice I had given him. Kirk said, "I am coming out to see Tom." Shortly later he arrived. I told all the reasons that this was not a good investment. It had some major risks that hadn't been told. Kirk left saying he wondered if he could get his other customers out of it.

A short time later, Claude Kirk ran for governor of Florida and won. Sometime later he called me and said he wanted me to be on the Florida Land Sales Board. There were some major problems with Gulf American Land. I thanked him. I said I knew very little about land sales and turned him down. He said, "Switch me up to Larry Lee."

Shortly after that, I got a call from Larry Lee. He said, "Congratulations, you are on the Florida Land Sales Board." Gulf

America Land was selling lots on the beach and then moving those sales into the swamp, and reselling the beach lots over and over.

We, the board, went to their office one Friday morning. When I was at the Harvard Business School, I majored in accounting under Professor Edmund Learner. He was considered the top accounting teacher in the country. At any rate, while going through Gulf's file, I was able to pull several documents that proved what they were doing.

Our group went to lunch and I showed the others on the R. E. Board the proof I had. When we went back after lunch, the head of the office said we were not allowed back in the building. Unfortunately the office burned down over the weekend and all the records were destroyed. We eventually put the company and Chairman Rosen out of business. Elliot Mackell was the president of Mackell Brothers, the company that developed Marco Island. He was on the Florida Land Sales Board with me.

In the meantime, someone had put sand in the gas tank of Elliot Mackell's airplane. He was able to land his plane, but it scared all of us. I had been called in by Rosen, and he offered me a job at triple my salary to run his family trusts.

At that time Mackay Shields, an investment management firm, had made me an excellent offer to join them in New York City. We had just had our second son, Peter. My wife, Posy, and I were very relieved to get away from the Florida Real Estate Board and Gulf America Land Co. We knew these guys weren't kidding. I was willing to risk my life to do the right thing, but once I was assured the company and chairman were out of business, I also had an obligation to my own family.

CHAPTER 21

The Boston Company

After leaving Jacksonville, I went to New York City with MacKay Shields, an investment advisory firm as senior vice president. Gil MacKay, the chairman, was a momentum investor, and we had a large number of corporate clients that used our advice for their pension plans. Bill Feick was the president. He was very aggressive, and on one client ski weekend, he took a swing at one of our clients. This made me very nervous.

At that time Vernon Alden had become chairman of the Boston Company. Vern had been a dean at the Harvard Business School when I was there. I was a roommate of his brother, Bert. I had become a good friend of Vern and Les Rollins. Les was also a dean at Harvard Business School. Vern had been recruited to become president of the University of Ohio and got Les Rollins to join him. After ten successful years, he later became the chairman of the Boston Company. *Time* magazine had written an article on Vern, who was putting together a "String of Pearls." Vern asked me to head up the Boston Company Institutional Investors to run pension funds. I decided I would do it.

The Boston Company office.
Your wife is calling and wondering why you
are not home for dinner on Sunday!

We did a terrific job for a number of years. We had Jerry
Zokowski as our insurance expert and had bought a stock called
Equity Funding. One afternoon, Jerry came in and said he had just
talked to his friend, an insurance expert, Raymond Dirks.

Dirks told Jerry that he had just come back from California
investigating a potential fraud rumor at Equity Funding and claimed
the company had tried to run over him in a car.

I said I was going to a Pension meeting at Allied Chemical in
NYC the next day and would like to see Dirks that morning. I did and
he told me the story about a man who had worked at Equity Funding
and was telling about the company keeping two sets of books. I asked
how long ago that man had left the company. Dirks said 28 months.
I knew that if someone left a company more than 24 months ago,
what he said was not inside information. I then called our lawyer

at Goodwin, Procter and Hoar and told him about Dirk's report. He agreed that we were not dealing with inside information and we could sell the stock. I went back and told my investment group that no matter what, there were too many negatives in the marketplace and we should sell the stock. My managers had the right to make the decisions on their accounts, and everyone but Grayson Murphy sold their positions. I told my group that Dirks said the former employee had met with the Chief Enforcement Officer, Stanley Sporkin, of the SEC, two weeks before I met with Dirks. Sporkin called a former SEC employee who had gone to work at Equity Funding and was told that the fraud information was from a former disgruntled employee, and Sporkin dropped the matter.

That weekend, Posy and I had gone out to a party. Her father had given her a little Triumph. When I went to drive it, I could not fit into the driver seat, so she drove. On the way home in a fierce rainstorm, the car slipped off the road and we crashed into a large tree. We were both in bad shape and were taken to the hospital. We were bandaged so that when my youngest son saw me, he said, "Are you my mother or my father?" That weekend the Equity Funding story hit the newspaper. I didn't get out of the hospital for over a week, and when I eventually went to the office, I got ahold of the report done by our lawyers on Equity Funding and there was no report of my call and conversation from NYC. Nate Garrick, a senior VP of the Boston Company, had earlier asked me if I wanted my own lawyer. I said no, I would use the Boston Company law firm, Goodwin, Proctor and Hoar. After I read this report and was told the SEC wanted to see me, Garrick again asked me if I wanted my own lawyer. I said absolutely! It turned out the lawyers at Goodwin were trying to say that our pension management group was independent of the Boston Company Management with separate shareholders. (We had 40 percent of the Boston Company Institutional Investors and the Boston Company owned the majority 60 percent.) I hired Bill Condren, my former Fordham friend and classmate. While I was at the Harvard Business School, Bill was at the Harvard Law School. Bill clarified all the positions so the SEC backed off our being an independent company. I was asked to go in and talk to Stanley Sporkin, the Chief Enforcement Officer of the SEC.

I sat down in his office and he said, "Did you believe this fraud story?" I said, "Did you?" He said, "I will ask the questions." I said, "No, I want to know if I am going to be held more responsible for the very information you, the Chief Enforcement Officer of the SEC, had been given two weeks earlier than I, from the same source." He turned red, and said, "You are right, get the hell out of here."

Had the Boston Company, in particular Bill Wolbach the president, succeeded in his effort, I could have been banned for life from the investment business.

Wolbach fired me and tried to welsh on my contract for my shares in the Boston Company Institutional Investors. If we were not able to agree on the contract, the agreement called for outside arbitration. We spent two years and all sorts of low-ball offers from the Boston Company. Bill Wolbach even hired Professor Pierson Hunt from the Harvard Business School. Hunt taught a finance course that his students, including me, called "sweaty palms." At his expert testimony, he was so ill prepared that he couldn't answer the first five questions I asked him. He left the meeting totally embarrassed. Vern Alden said to give us what the contract provided. On one Friday afternoon, I got a call from the Boston Company, and they offered me less than one-third of what the contract required. I was working in Pittsburgh, Pennsylvania, as president of Federated Investment Counseling. I was worn out and tempted to take the offer. I said I would discuss it with my wife.

Tom and Posy with Marion and Vern Alden in Hawaii.

Tom and Vern were Trustees for the Hawaiian Tax Free Funds.

When I discussed it with Posy, she said they know something or wouldn't be calling me. I called them back on Monday and said I would not accept their offer. It turned out later that the arbitrator had called them earlier that week and was awarding us the full amount of our contract. I was awarded what the contract required, which was three times what Wolbach had offered on the previous Friday.

CHAPTER 22

Squam Lake—Two Vacations '81–'82

In 1975 our family went to Squam Lake for a vacation. I ran into Tom Gerache. Tom went to Fordham with me and was captain of the tennis team. He lived in Short Hills, New Jersey, a town next to Livingston, and sometimes he would give me a ride home on holidays. I had been playing tennis and asked Tom to play at Squam. I guess I didn't do that well, because Tom ducked me at the courts the remainder of the week.

At our forty-fifth reunion, I saw Tom was attending, so I called him and challenged him to a tennis match. He said sure and then forgot to bring his racquet. Five years later, I called and asked him to play at our fiftieth reunion. We set a date and the time and he said okay. Word got around that we were playing and Lang Toland, a classmate of mine, set up betting on the match. Tom Gerache was a 19 to 1 favorite. Gerache had recently won the New Jersey 70 and over tennis title. Only Lang and I bet on me. The next day I was there on time and warmed up with another classmate, Ed Walsh. Tom Gerache didn't show. Tom was an hour late when he arrived. I asked if he would like to warm up. He said no and we played. I won 6-0, 6-3, which stunned me. Tom said he would like to play at our fifty-fifth reunion, but it never took place. We never played at our sixtieth. I guess we will have to give it a try at our sixty-fifth.

In 1978 our family went back to Squam Lake for a week. The sports director asked if I would run in a camp relay race. There were two teams, and she put me on the weaker team. I was to run the last lap against a young college half-miler. When it came down to the last lap around a half-mile field, my team was ahead. I asked the young college runner to switch teams with me, and he did. I took off about 50 yards back. I picked up about 40 yards, but I was getting tired. I could see Posy and my three boys screaming for me to pass him. I tried to do it, but he started to sprint. I realized he might beat me, but I made a last effort. As we got to the finish line, he lunged for the tape, but he fell on the ground, short of the tape. Posy had clapped so hard that the face of her watch flew into the bushes. For me it was exciting since my family had never seen me run a race.

CHAPTER 23

A Tribute to Artie O'Conner in 2017

N orb Sander, the head of the New York City Armory 163 Street, was hosting a new event to honor the former Fordham track coach, Artie O'Conner. He asked me to write something about my coach. I wrote the following.

Artie O'Connor was an inspiration to me. Without saying anything, his attitude toward me was extremely important. He took my losses harder than I did. He shared my victories in a modest but in an enthusiastic fashion.

In my senior year I was going to run the Indoor IC4A 1000 yards against Arnie Sowell. At the Track Writers luncheon, he moved me into the 600 and told me I had a better chance to win the 600. That was a turning point in my running career. I was so disappointed I couldn't sleep that week. By the end of the week, I lost the 600 to Charlie Jenkins of Villanova but made a decision that I would beat Sowell. I ran every workout with a new dedication that I didn't understand myself. I'm not sure if Coach O'Connor meant to motivate me that way, but he did. I was going to beat Arnie Sowell and prove Coach O'Connor wrong.

Before I went to Los Angeles for the Olympic Trials, Artie told me, "Tom, three men qualify for the 800 on the Olympic Team. Stay in there and make the team."

That week after I had qualified for the 800 meters at the All-Service Championships, I decided to try to also qualify for the 400 meters in the AAU Championships. I ran and broke the U.S. Record. Artie called and said, "Forget what I said! Go out there and win the 800 in the trials." I did. And I set a new U.S. record.

I went to Australia and won the Melbourne Olympic 800 meters with a new Olympic record. When I came back to the United States, Artie said, "I knew you could do it." I looked at Artie and with a large smile I said, "Not without your help."

God bless you and thank you, Artie.

Norb died this year, shortly after the Artie O'Conner Meet. Norb had been a runner at Fordham University. He was a member of the 4-Mile Relay team that broke the Penn Relays record, and won the New York Marathon. He did a terrific thing establishing the 168th Street Armory. He had meets six days a week for three and a half months in the winter. He was reestablishing indoor track for the high schools in NYC. I and many, many track friends will greatly miss you.

CHAPTER 24

Eric Segal at Harvard

Bill McCurdy, the Harvard head track coach, came over to Eric Segal in the locker room. He said, "Eric, you have been on the track team for four years as a miler, and you have never broken five minutes. You have two weeks to do it. If not, I am taking away your locker and your uniform." My locker was next to Eric's. McCurdy added, "If you have anything to say, tell Tom. He will decide if I should know about it." Eric was unusual. He graduated summa cum laude at Harvard. He gave the graduation valedictorian speech in Greek so his critics couldn't find fault with his Latin. He had never taken a course in Greek.

Eric said to me, "What will I do?" I reminded him he had two weeks and should go out each day and pace himself to break five minutes. He did that but could not break the five minutes. He tried each day, but he could not break the five-minute mile. One day before his two weeks ended, he came in and started to weep. I said I would go out with him and pace him. He had to promise to stay with me. He did and ran 4.57 that day. He was elated. Later when he wrote *Love Story*, he sent me a copy and signed it, "800 Meters of Love. Eric."

Earlier he had tried to fix me up with the real Jennifer in Love Story. She went to Radcliffe and was in his class. He had tried to ask her out but she said, "Sorry, Preppie." He then said he knew she would like to go out with me. She said I should give her a call.

At Radcliffe the girls had a board for their phone messages. Each girl had a long nail on the board. When Eric told me about her messages, I strolled over in the late evening, close to the 11:00 p.m. curfew, to the message board. I saw her nail. It was stacked with two inches of messages. I pulled the messages off her nail and put mine on it. The next day she called me and I asked her out on a date. She said yes. I suppose it stunned her to have only one message the night before. She was just like the Jennifer in the book. She was beautiful, thought Babe Ruth was a candy bar, and called me Preppie during the entire date. I did not leave any more messages on her nail.

Eric wrote several best-sellers, including *The Class* and *Jonathan Livingston Seagull*. He went down to teach at Yale.

He also ran some marathons. The TV station covering the Boston Marathon asked him to wear a camera on his head while he ran in the race. I went to see him run and was positioned myself very near the finish. As Eric ran by, I called out, "Hello, Eric." He looked over to see me and stepped in a pothole and fell down. When he got up, he had trouble going forward. Although his time wasn't that good, after 26 miles, a fall was a difficult proposition. Finally he got going. I ran around to the finish line where I caught him. I said I was sorry for distracting him and causing him to fall. He said, "Are you kidding? Did you hear how the crowd cheered as I again got running?"

Eric later moved his family to England.

We exchanged letters as the years went by, and I missed him when he passed away.

Ron Delany, 1500-Meter Olympic Champion

R on won the 1500 meters in the 1956 Olympics. He was the best in the world at 1500 meters and the mile. He was also a heck of a good half-miler. We raced against one another four times. I felt I could beat him if I stayed next to him during the race because I was faster than Ron. I had won the AAU Championships at 400 meters in an American record. I ran against him at the Coliseum Relays and won the race. Later after a protest by Mal Whitfield, they declared the second- place man, Ron Delany, the winner. Then again in the Nationals I won. I knew if I ran to win, I could do it.

In the other two races, Ron had already run and won the mile. I decided I could hold back and outkick him at the finish. But I thought what that would mean to me. The answer was that I was at the point where I felt I would have very few opportunities to go for the world record, and this was one of them. I went out fast and built up a 40-yard lead on the field, including Ron, but I died on the final straightaway. Ron nipped me at the tape. I gave my all and thought the effort was worth it.

I knew I was coming near the end of my running. I had run a relay leg in 1.43 at the Penn Relays. I started behind about 60 yards. I was relaxed and ran in a freewheeling way for the entire half mile. I felt if I could relax the way I did in that race, I might be able to break the current world record of 1.47 by a wide margin, and establish a record that would stand for a long time I knew the pace I had to run, and in the Texas meets I hit that pace for the 220, the 440, and the 660. If I could finish, I potentially could cut 4 or 5 seconds off the world record. I knew relaxation was the key, but the excitement of the race overcame me and my 40 yards disappeared.

Later I talked to Ron and said he owed it to himself and the other competitors to go for the world record, instead of just trying to win the race. He said, "Tom, I am a young man and have plenty of time to do that." I said, "Ron, two years from now some guy you have never heard of will beat you by ten yards." Two years later we were together. He had lost to Herb Elliott. He said, "Tom, that was two years, but it was twenty yards, not ten."

Charlie Jenkins, 400-Meter Olympic Champion

The summer after the Melbourne Olympics, I was on a European trip with Charlie Jenkins, the 400-meter winner of the Olympics. I told Charlie I wanted to have a 400 race with him. The next meet I signed up to run the 400. Then Charlie signed up to run the 800.

I told Charlie in the next meet I had signed up for the 200 meters, 400 meters, 800 meters, and the 1500 meters. Whatever he was going to run, I would be in that race. The next meet was in Bislett Stadium, in Oslo, Norway, one of the fastest tracks in Europe. We ran the 400 meters. I was in the third lane, and Charlie was in the fifth lane. I won the race in 45 seconds. Charlie was in second place at the finish.

I still talk to Charlie. He and his son, Chip, were one of the few father-and-son Olympians. They both went to Villanova. Charlie was in the State Department and later one of the top managers in the Social Security Department.

1957 Tom setting new US Record in 400 meters, in Bislet Stadium, Oslo, Norway.

Charlie Jenkins was second on outside.

CHAPTER 27

Mugged in New York City

W hen I was working in New York, I used to work out at the New York Athletic Club. I had run on the NYAC track team for a number of years. Each year the club had the NY Police Department give a self-defense course in the gym. I took the course a number of times. It was a great course and taught me how to respond to a mugger's attack.

We were inducted into the NYAC Hall of Fame.

L to R Ray Lump, Horace Ashenfelter. Tom Courtney, Lindy Remigino, Alice Landon (representing husband Dick), Ray Barbutti, Al Oerter, Doug Blubough, Bob Clotworthey and Alan Helfrich.

One night I was returning to the NYAC at 58th Street. I had just gone in a deli and bought a sandwich and a carton of milk. I was one block away from the NYAC and suddenly three men attacked me. One grabbed me from behind my neck, the second punched me in my right side, and the third reached into my back pocket for my wallet. Instantly I thought of the story my son told me how his teacher's brother had been mugged in NYC, had his head bashed down onto the sidewalk, and he was never the same again.

I erupted, turning to my left, and smashed the nose of the man behind me. The man with his hand in my back pocket was pulled under my body, and I heard a loud scream as his arm was shattered under my weight. The third man ran down the road. I got up and sprinted after him and tackled him at the corner of the NYAC. Somehow there was a policeman right there to help me. He grabbed the man, and I explained what had just happened. We went back to where the other two men had been lying, but other than blood all over the sidewalk, they were gone.

The man we caught was heavily doped out. They took him to the police station. He refused to identify the other two. He eventually was sent to jail for three years for mugging, attempted robbery, and not identifying his partners. I was happy to have survived. My wife said his friends might try to seek revenge on me and my family since the attack was a matter of public record.

As my dad always said, if someone starts the fight, you have the obligation, if possible, to end it. In this case, public record or not, I had to try help prosecute such behavior. Everyone has an obligation to help one another.

CHAPTER 28

President Father Joseph O'Hare S.J.

F ather O'Hare was the president of Fordham for twenty years. He attended the 1996 Olympics in Atlanta. I had obtained forty tickets at the finish of the 800-meter final and asked him to invite Fordham people to attend. We had a cocktail party hosted by Georgia Pacific on the fortieth floor in their building that overlooked the Olympic Stadium. We showed the film of my 800-meter victory in the Melbourne Olympics. We then went down to watch the 800 final of the 1996 Atlanta Olympics. Later Father O'Hare said it was exciting to watch but nothing compared to the film of my race that we saw at the reception.

Posy and Tom at the 1996 Atlanta Olympics in front of
Peter Calaboyias' larger than life sculpture that saved the
lives of several people from the Mad Bomber's Explosion.

The three figures represent an ancient Olympian, a
modern day Olympian and a female in the Olympics.

Sometime later Father O'Hare said to me, "Tom, take care of
yourself." I said thank you. He said, "No, I mean it, take care of
yourself." I said, "Thank you again, but why are you stressing it?"
He said, "Tom, of the original five men that were inducted into the
Fordham Hall of Fame, you are the only one still alive." The other
four were Vince Lombardi, Frankie Frish, Alex Wojciechowicz, and
Jack Coffee. All had passed away.

Twenty years later that was a distinction I wanted to maintain.

CHAPTER 29

President Joseph M. McShane, S.J.

I decided to go to Fordham University without ever seeing the school. Today no one would do that. I was offered a full scholarship. My mother thought it was wonderful. Her favorite cousin, Charles Dubell, had been captain of the Fordham Track Team and loved the school. I saw the school the night before class started in 1951. Artie O'Conner, the track coach, played an important role in my track career. Cardinal Avery Dullas was one of my philosophy teachers. My roommates in Martyrs Court—Bob Mackin, Jack Dash, Carl Candels, Jack Kenally, and Jack Stanton—remain close friends. Ruppert Wentworth, my roommate, died of cancer a few years ago, but I will always remember him as a true friend.

Fordham has been exceptionally graced with Father McShane as its president for the past thirteen years. He had been the president of Scranton University. When he came to Fordham, he laid out his plans and dreams. He said in the 1930s, Fordham had been the number one Catholic college in the United States, and his goal was to return it to that place again. Year after year he has made major progress, and although not number one yet, Fordham is getting closer every year. Every Fordham student and graduate can be proud of the job Father McShane is doing.

CHAPTER 30

Bill Condren

I mentioned how Bill Condren met me the night I arrived at Fordham and carried my suitcase up to my room in the dormitory. I assumed he was an upperclassman. The next day I went to my first class and there was Bill. We became good friends, and when I went up to the Harvard Business School, Bill went to the Harvard Law School.

When I later ran into some legal problems, Bill agreed to help me. He did a terrific job.

Even when he got into the jet plane leasing business on a full-time basis, he still would represent me. He was very successful in the leasing business. He took a very small fee up front, but ended up with the planes after twenty years. As it turned out, the planes were worth more after twenty years than the original cost. Bill made a fortune!!

Bill went into horseracing and won the Kentucky Derby several times with Strike the Gold, Go for Gin, and Louis Quatorze.

When I was at Fordham, we had an outdoor track. When the school built the new athletic complex called the Lombardi Center, the track team lost its outdoor track. The new complex did include a flat-floor 200-meter indoor track, a new major swimming pool, and many training facilities. Fordham did not have sufficient land to rebuild the outdoor 400-meter track.

At one of our reunions Bill and I talked about the possibility of putting in a 400-meter track on the top of the new parking garage that Fordham was building. I looked into the building of such a facility. Georgetown had put up a track on a garage. The AAU office had some ideas to help us. Craig Masback, a terrific Princeton miler and a friend of my son, Tom, had become the head of the AAU and was anxious to help because he thought it would reinvigorate track in the New York City area.

I put together all the information, and estimates on cost, etc., and had a preliminary study done to see how the extension of the top of the garage could handle the track and spectators.

Bill was going to put in the bulk of the funds, and I was going to spearhead the drive to get matching gifts. The university decided we would be competing for alumnae funds, and turned down our plan. Fordham had decided that they could only afford a major effort for football, basketball, and baseball and would run the other sports programs on a far more limited basis.

Unfortunately Bill died a short time later, and the indoor 400-meter track died with him.

Mal Whitfield

Mal Whitfield was a great runner. He won the 800-meter run in the 1948 and 1952 Olympics. He held the half-mile world record. Indoors he sometimes would win the 600 yards and the 1000 yards in the same evening.

The first time I saw him at a meet, I went over to say hello and tell him how much I admired him. He looked at me with a blank stare and walked away without saying a word. Someone said that was the way he concentrated.

The first time I ran against him was in the 1955 Coliseum Relays half-mile. I walked over and wished him luck. He did not acknowledge me and walked away. I ran and won the race. He claimed I interfered with his race and that I barged into him and Arnie Sowell. I never saw either Whitfield or Sowell during the race, but because he was such a bigshot, the judges accepted his story and disqualified me. They gave the first place to the second-place man, Ron Delany.

At the outdoor national championship that year, I was racing in the finals of the half-mile. Whitfield was next to me. He purposely faked a start and I stepped over the line and was disqualified.

In the Olympic Trials, Mal was in the finals with me. He made his move to the front with a half lap to go just the way he had done in his previous Olympic victories. I went right after him and sailed by. At the finish, he ended up in fifth place and did not make the

Olympic team. I went over to say hello after the race, and he turned away without even letting me say anything.

It was interesting that he had run 1.49 to win the 1948 Olympics. He ran 1.49 to win the 1952 Olympics and the identical 1.49 to take fifth in the 1956 Olympic Trials.

When I went on my first European trip, I was told by our Finnish host that Mal Whitfield had been banned from visiting Finland because of his bad behavior. After that I decided that I didn't need to say hello to him in the future and I did not.

It does not take a lot of effort to be nice. Mal tried to intimidate his opponents. He may have had some success with that, but in the end, despite his outstanding running success, he had very few friends. I know I was not one of them.

Letter to Don Bowden

This is the letter I wrote to Don Bowden in 2007 when *Track & Field News* was celebrating Don being the first American to break the four-minute mile. John Hendershott asked me to write a letter to Don.

To Jon Hendershott, publisher of *Track & Field* magazine:

Dear Don,
It was wonderful to hear *Track & Field News* is having a fiftieth anniversary for you being the first American to break the sub 4:00 minute mile.
Two weeks before your race, I worked out with you at the University of California. You said we should work out on the Cal grass track because it would be refreshing for our legs. This was just five days before I was going to try to break 4 minutes at Modesto. We ran a 3/4 mile in 2.58. Having never run on a grass track, I did not realize it was such a different surface, and when we finished, I was exhausted. A month earlier I ran a 3/4 mile clocked by Coach Johnny Morris at Houston University in 2:52 and felt ready to

run another lap. I know you didn't intend it, but when I ran on Saturday, I had lost my confidence and never went with the pacesetter as I had planned. Then the following week you ran a 3.58 at Stockton. I went back to the 880 yards and did break the world record a few weeks later at the Coliseum, but my mile days were over. To this day I know that you are such a wonderful gentleman that you never suggested that grass workout with any ulterior motive.

We were on the same 1956 Olympic team, but you were suffering from mono, and never had the chance you deserved. You did get that chance at Stockton, and I want to send my sincere congratulations for a super effort. When I come out to California this year, I am having Lon Spurrier set up a mile race for the three of us—on a good rubber track and let's see what happens.

Love,
Tom Courtney

CHAPTER 33

Sports Illustrated, Roy Campanella

Sports Illustrated put me on their cover in 1955 and again in 1956, the latter being a painter's impression of the 800 meters Olympic final. I also did sports clinics for *Sports Illustrated*. Keith Morris was the head of promotions and I participated in clinics and similar meetings.

One time we went over to visit with Dodger catcher Roy Campanella at his home. Roy had been in a bad auto accident and was paralyzed and confined to a wheelchair. While talking to him, I asked who the fastest pitcher he had ever caught. I figured it would be Rex Barney. He said I would never have heard of him.

Now to retrace an incident, some of my friends and I were at the Chanticleer Restaurant in Millburn, New Jersey, and we got in a discussion with another group. They said their man, Ed Burke (he had a patch on one eye), was the fastest pitcher in the world. My group said I had the fastest ball in town. Well, we made a bet and went out in the parking lot. Both our cars had gloves and baseballs. He would fire his pitch to me, and then I would throw my pitch to him. The group would decide the winner. Burke threw his pitch and as it came to me, it suddenly shot upward. Somehow I managed to catch it, but I felt very lucky it didn't take my head off. I then threw my pitch and Joe Zahn and my buddies all cheered and each side claimed victory. Only the power of cheering from my friends made this contest a draw.

Campanella said he was on spring practice in Florida and this young guy with a patch on one eye threw him a pitch. The pitch was so fast when it zoomed upward, Campy missed it and it sank into a palm tree right behind him. He said I can't remember his full name, but his first name was Ed. I said Ed Burke. Campanella could not believe it when I told him. He said, "The world is a small place, isn't it."

CHAPTER 34

Running for the Train

At age forty-two, I was leaving my office at the Boston Company building to walk to the train station, about a mile. I was jogging when I started to pass a young 20-year-old man also jogging. As I went by him, he moved smartly by me, and so I picked up my pace and started to move by him again. He then took off like a shot, and we repeated the previous exchange. As I passed him (carrying my briefcase), he set into a full sprint and I did the same. We raced down the street to the RR station where we both stopped, with me holding a slight lead. Just before I boarded the train to Concord, he ran over and said, "Do you take this train every day? If so, I will see you tomorrow. I want another shot at you."

CHAPTER 35

Lucky to Have Strong Legs

T his is a story Posy said to tell. We were living in a home in Concord, Massachusetts, in 1970. The house was on the top of Nashawtuc Hill and had been designed by Andrew Hepburn, one of the two architects that redesigned Williamsburg. We had a big property, and I had bought a large powerful sit-down mower so I could mow our lawn myself. I was going up a very steep hill when the mower tipped over backward. I never expected it and ended up with the mower on top of me supported by my legs. I tried to call for help, but no one heard me. While I debated what to do, I felt the oil dripping down on me and the motor was still running. Now I realized with a hot motor, this could explode on me. With every ounce of strength, I pushed my legs and the new mower went sailing backward over my head. As Posy used to say, "It's good to have strong legs, and someone else to mow the lawn."

CHAPTER 36

Trinidad the Savannah

I was working in Trinidad, looking at some investments we had made. We were staying at a hotel, which adjoined the savannah. I went out to take a jog and saw four men training. I asked them if I could work out with them. They were running in and out 400s. Each man led his 400. After 4x400, they said, "Okay, man let's see you do your 400." I bolted out and ran my 400. The leader of the group said, "Who are you, man?"

We chatted about the Melbourne Olympics. Those four runners were the Trinidad Relay team. Later that evening at my hotel, they brought over a book on their athletic club and asked me to sign it. They also gave me a CD of their most popular singer, the Sparrow.

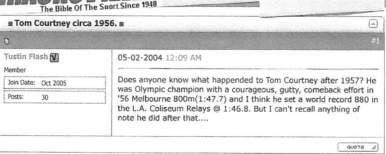

Tom Courtney circa 1956.

#1

Tustin Flash
Member
Join Date: Oct 2005
Posts: 30

05-02-2004 12:09 AM

Does anyone know what happended to Tom Courtney after 1957? He was Olympic champion with a courageous, gutty, comeback effort in '56 Melbourne 800m(1:47.7) and I think he set a world record 880 in the L.A. Coliseum Relays @ 1:46.8. But I can't recall anything of note he did after that....

QUOTE

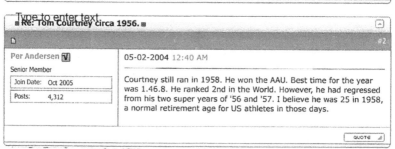

Type to enter text

Re: Tom Courtney circa 1956.

#2

Per Andersen
Senior Member
Join Date: Oct 2005
Posts: 4,312

05-02-2004 12:40 AM

Courtney still ran in 1958. He won the AAU. Best time for the year was 1.46.8. He ranked 2nd in the World. However, he had regressed from his two super years of '56 and '57. I believe he was 25 in 1958, a normal retirement age for US athletes in those days.

QUOTE

Re: Tom Courtney circa 1956.

#3

jhc68
Senior Member
Join Date: Oct 2005
Posts: 3,316

05-02-2004 01:34 AM

Hey, Tustin Flash! Wasn't it Tom Courtney's Olympic run that our high school coach had a recording about? It was Bob Richards describing that gutty, aching run to the finish... remember that? Take care.

QUOTE

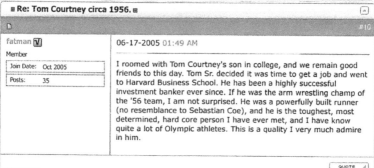

Re: Tom Courtney circa 1956.

#10

fatman
Member
Join Date: Oct 2005
Posts: 35

06-17-2005 01:49 AM

I roomed with Tom Courtney's son in college, and we remain good friends to this day. Tom Sr. decided it was time to get a job and went to Harvard Business School. He has been a highly successful investment banker ever since. If he was the arm wrestling champ of the '56 team, I am not surprised. He was a powerfully built runner (no resemblance to Sebastian Coe), and he is the toughest, most determined, hard core person I have ever met, and I have know quite a lot of Olympic athletes. This is a quality I very much admire in him.

QUOTE

care, jnc

QUOTE

Re: Tom Courtney circa 1956.
#4

hj197steve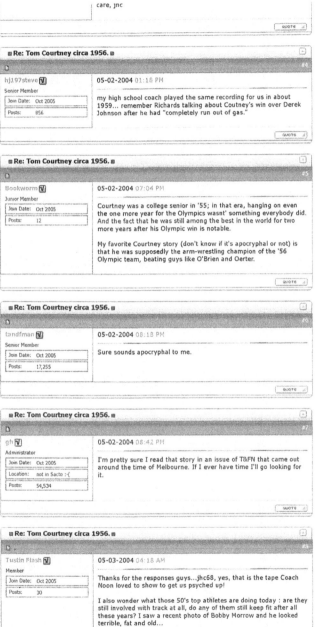
Senior Member
Join Date: Oct 2005
Posts: 856

05-02-2004 01:16 PM

my high school coach played the same recording for us in about 1959... remember Richards talking about Coutney's win over Derek Johnson after he had "completely run out of gas."

QUOTE

Re: Tom Courtney circa 1956.
#5

Bookworm
Junior Member
Join Date: Oct 2005
Posts: 12

05-02-2004 07:04 PM

Courtney was a college senior in '55; in that era, hanging on even the one more year for the Olympics wasnt' something everybody did. And the fact that he was still among the best in the world for two more years after his Olympic win is notable.

My favorite Courtney story (don't know if it's apocryphal or not) is that he was supposedly the arm-wrestling champion of the '56 Olympic team, beating guys like O'Brien and Oerter.

QUOTE

Re: Tom Courtney circa 1956.
#6

tandfman
Senior Member
Join Date: Oct 2005
Posts: 17,255

05-02-2004 08:18 PM

Sure sounds apocryphal to me.

QUOTE

Re: Tom Courtney circa 1956.
#7

gh
Administrator
Join Date: Oct 2005
Location: not in Sacto :-(
Posts: 54,534

05-02-2004 08:42 PM

I'm pretty sure I read that story in an issue of T&FN that came out around the time of Melbourne. If I ever have time I'll go looking for it.

QUOTE

Re: Tom Courtney circa 1956.
#8

Tustin Flash
Member
Join Date: Oct 2005
Posts: 30

05-03-2004 04:18 AM

Thanks for the responses guys...jhc68, yes, that is the tape Coach Noon loved to show to get us psyched up!

I also wonder what those 50's top athletes are doing today : are they still involved with track at all, do any of them still keep fit after all these years? I saw a recent photo of Bobby Morrow and he looked terrible, fat and old...

Paul Anderson and Track & Field News

While I was at the Boston Army Base, I had an arm wrestling match with Harold Connolly. He was the national champion in the hammer throw. He worked out at Harvard. Harold and I had this match. I won it. He couldn't believe it and said he wanted a rematch. Harold had broken his left arm as a child and built up his right arm so it was huge. This gave him a decided advantage in the hammer since it shortened his turn with the left side and accelerated his right side. He held the world record, and won the Olympics.

Still, he wanted a rematch with me. He set up matches with others at the Olympics but lost them. Al Hall from Cornell was second in the hammer. He lost his match with me. Finally Harold said, "If you lose the next match I arrange, you will give me a rematch." He set up a match with Paul Anderson, the strongest man in the world. Paul came over to my room at the Olympic Village and challenged me. I said I would give him one try, but not that day. The day Paul was to compete in the finals of his event, I went over to his room and put my arm on the table and said, "Okay, Paul, let's go." He said, "It's my finals today for the title of the World's Strongest Heavyweight Lifter and I can't do it." That afternoon after he won his event, he ran over to my room and said, "Okay, Courtney, put your arm on the table. I am going to break it off." I said, "Sorry, Paul, you had your one chance." He went crazy. Harold never got his rematch.

The preceding pages were from the files at *Track & Field* News. It was sent to me, and I thought you might be interested in it.

Years later my dad was reading this, and he asked me if anyone had defeated me in arm wrestling. I said, "No." Now my older brother, Jim, was there and he said he had never lost an arm wrestling match. He was certain he could beat me. Well, my dad said, "Let's see." Neither Jim nor I would give in. After a long time, I slammed his arm to the floor. Jim had torn the ligaments off his elbow.

CHAPTER 38

Values and Religion

The following is a letter I wrote to my brother-in-law, Gilbert Dunham. He is Abby's husband, who is Posy's identical twin sister. Gil was a graduate of Princeton and had his law degree from Columbia. We had had a number of conversations on the above topic, and I tried to summarize my thoughts to him and I have enclosed them.

Tom and Brother in Law Gil Dunham at Fallingwater
designed by architect Frank Lloyd Wright in Pennsylvania.

Posy and Abby, Posy's twin, at Place des Vosges, Paris, France

Values and Religion 6/28/08

Tom W. Courtney

What is my personal evidence of Christ?

In 1987 in Medjugorje, Yugoslavia, my family and I met with Maria Popovich. She was one of the six apparitionists who were seeing and meeting with the Blessed Mother Mary every day. We were staying at Jozo Vasil's home. He was our taxi driver and had driven us from Dubrovnik to Medjugorje. He was also a cousin of Maria's. He agreed to try to set up a meeting with her for us. He said to bring an interpreter for she spoke no English. She had just graduated from the local high school. Jozo set the meeting with Maria. I tried to find an interpreter but was unable to find one.

Maria in Medjugorie with all five of us.

L to R Frank, Peter, Posy, Tom, Maria, Tom jr.

We knocked on her door and she motioned us to come in. She talked to us in perfect English for an hour and twenty minutes. I also played my tape recorder and video camera during our visit. Later when I tried to play them back, I discovered nothing on them. When Maria said it was very important to go to a priest for confession, my son, Tom, said he went directly to God for his confession. She said, "No, Jesus set up confession with his Apostles. 'Whose sins you shall forgive, they are forgiven. Whose sins you shall retain, they are retained.' It was important to do what Jesus asked."

Later when we climbed Mount Krizevac, Posy smelled roses. This was a sign that the Blessed Mother was giving her blessings. In 1988 Posy, our son, Frank, and I went to Medjugore again. I met Maria and she could only speak Croatian. On the night of a special feast for the Virgin Mary, Frank saw the concrete cross on Mount Krizevac light up. Several thousand other visitors also saw it. I noticed the chain in my rosary had turned from silver to gold.

In 1989 Jan Connell, a good friend of ours, was asked by Jesus to bring fifty people to Medjugorje to celebrate His Mother's birthday on August 5 (not September 8, the date the church recognizes). When I had decided to go on my first trip to Medjugorje, it was with my family, and I felt compelled to go. I did not intend to go the second time, but when asked by Jan, I felt compelled again and went with Posy and my son, Frank. We had a wonderful trip but decided that was it. In 1989, Jan said she had forty-nine people to make the trip. I can't tell you why, but I had to accept and be the fiftieth person.

I went alone to Medjugorje with the forty-nine other people from Pittsburgh.

Our group included five youths, ten to twelve years old. They saw the Blessed Mother appear and speak to the apparitionists at the Saint James choir loft. The rest of our group saw nothing. Back at our hotel we listened separately to each youth, and what they described was identical.

Posy in front of Courtney's Tavern in Kilarney, Ireland.
I bought a round of drinks for everyone at the bar at 10 AM.

In the Loire Valley, France.

Posy and Tom pretended this was their summer
home, Chateau Azay le Rideau.

In 2000 Posy and I met Lilian Bernas, a "victim soul" whom
Jesus has given the gift of the stigmata (the five wounds of Christ),
which manifest fully on Good Friday. At Saint Elizabeth Seton
Church in Naples, we saw and tape-recorded Lilian bleeding. Posy
smelled lilies in our home in Florida when Lilian and her adopted

parents had dinner with us. Our son, Peter, felt a special warmth from their hands when they said some prayers for him. He had been suffering from a bad back caused by a rear-end auto crash.

In 2008 Posy and I saw Lilian's welts on her hands a short time before Good Friday. We again saw her bleed from all of her wounds. Intellectuals may accept Darwin's theory, but that is all it is. The scientific community doesn't believe that man possesses a soul whose essence is divine. Avery Dulles, son of John Foster Dulles, converted to Catholicism and became a Jesuit priest. His father, John Foster Dulles, disowned him. Later his father made amends with his son. He was one of my philosophy teachers at Fordham. He became a cardinal and the church accepted him as one of the world's greatest philosophers, and he did not accept the scientific community.

Man has an innate calling from God. Jesus said you must come through Him, with His Grace to get to heaven. Man can accept this Grace or reject it. People who reject His Grace justify this rejection in the guise of science and the fact that they cannot observe it. God does not want man to be lonely or too pompous, but that seems to be the fate of most rejecters. I pray every day that all these scientific intellectuals will accept God's Grace. On their deathbeds, I hope they will say, "I don't deserve it, but please give me Your Grace!"

Unless a person can find satisfactory answers to the questions of why I exist, why must I suffer, why is there evil and at death, what happens to me, his life, no matter how successful, becomes meaningless. A person can only answer these problems in a religion. Catholicism claims it alone is the true religion founded by Christ. Remember that the Apostles spent most of three years with Christ before he was crucified, died, and rose from the dead. These men *all* died as martyrs rather than deny Christ. Christ said He would be with His church until the end of time. He is!

(Mrs.) Beth D. Rickman
10 Linden Drive
Kingston, RI   02881
(401) 782-0792
October 1, 1997

This is a letter from a gratefull daughter that might interest you.

Mr. Tom Courtney
P. O. Box 580
Sewickley, PA 15143

Dear Mr. Courtney:

This is a thank-you letter, albeit forty years after the fact, on behalf of my Dad, George I. Davis of Glens Falls, NY. Dad passed away in January 1996, and while going through some of his personal possessions this past week, I found a ticket stub from the Olympic tryouts of Saturday, June 30, 1956, 2:00 PM, at the L. A. Coliseum. Your name was written in pencil on the back, which is what prompted me to try to find you.

I wrote Steve Harris, a friend who has recently written a book on Olympic medalists for the U. S. Olympic organization. He passed my letter on to Barry King's office, whose associate called to give me your address.

As best as my recollection serves me, Dad told us that he had met you in the lobby of an L. A. hotel. Apparently your own father was not able to see you run on June 30th, so you gave Dad his ticket. Dad went to see you run and was so proud that you won. I've often wondered if you recalled meeting Dad and giving him this ticket.

Do you remember hearing about the two planes that collided over the Grand Canyon in 1956, at least one of them a commercial plane? Dad had been booked home on the commercial plane that crashed, but because of his "chance" encounter with you, he cancelled his seat on that ill-fated flight. Until the day Dad died he carried part of that stub in his wallet, and we buried that stub and several other meaningful items with him.

I don't know if Dad ever was in touch with you or not, and over the years I have to admit I forgot your name. But when I found the other half of the ticket with your name on the back, I just wanted to write to tell you this story and to thank you for giving Dad the ticket and for giving us Dad for another forty years.

Dad was a successful insurance executive, a humble man who kept the company of both the great and the lowly with equal ease, a loving and inspiring father, a leader in his community and at several colleges and universities, and one whose lifelong belief was concern for others. He believed his forty extra years to have been a gift and always did his best to leave things better than he had found them. I know you would have liked Dad. On behalf of all of us who loved him so dearly, thanks for the ticket and the extra years.

WITH DEEPEST APPRECIATION,

Beth R—

Oct. 10, 1987

Dear Beth,

I remember your Dad giving me a congratulatory hug after the meet. He said he was very proud of me, and that I would win the Olympics. I was surprised by his enthusiasm. When I had met him at the hotel, he struck me as a quiet man, much like my dad. What I remember the most was that when I arrived home, my Dad hugged me (which he rarely ever did) and told me I would win the Olympics. It was eerie!

Today I know nothing happens by accident. I don't pretend to understand why our Lord operates the way He does.

After the Olympics, I went to the Harvard Business School and was very successful in the investment business. My success consumed me and I developed a big head that nearly destroyed me and my family. In 1987 I was invited to go to Medjugorje, Yugoslavia, and felt compelled to go. While there my three sons and I visited with one of the visionaries, Maria. We talked at her home for an hour and twenty minutes in English. We found out later that she spoke no English. I went back a year later to confirm this for myself. It was true! I went back the next year to thank the Lord and his Mother Mary.

I have enclosed an article on Father Scheier who spoke at the Pittsburgh Marian Conference I attended this past September 6. I believe the Lord interceded in your dad's life to allow him to show his concern for others for another forty years. God bless you, and keep up your Dad's good works.

Sincerely in Christ,
Tom Courtney

Another Gift in My Life.

This is a letter I wrote to my mother about Father Bernard and his church in Donora, Pennsylvania.

4/30/89

Dear Mom,

As you can see from the enclosed article Holy Trinity Church is receiving lots of attention. I was at this last Friday's service and it was attended by over 500. After the service, a group went to Eat N' Park and we discussed the cures that were taking place at a church in Donora, Pa. On Saturday I decided to go to Mass at Holy Name of the Blessed Virgin Mary Church in Donora, Pa.

After Mass I talked to the Pastor Fr. Bernard Kaczmarzyk. He told me that in 1975 he made his first trip out of this country to Rome. He had recently been made Pastor in Donora. A priest friend made him promise to visit Fr. Gino. Father Gino is a stigmatist and received this blessing at the deathbed of Padre Pio who had the stigmata.

Fr. Bernard encountered all sorts of problems getting to meet Fr. Gino, but was finally told he and his group would visit for 10 minutes. When he lined up first to introduce his group, he was told to go to the end of the line. Fr. Gino "sees hearts" and Father Bernard thought he saw something unfavorable. When they finally met, Fr. Gino kissed his hands and blessed him. Fr. Bernard passed out cold. Later Fr. Gino told him that the Blessed Mother would be present at a shrine in his church in Donora.

Donora was a very poor parish and when the architect/artist said he could make a shrine at the altar for $250,000, Fr. Bernard knew he could not do it. Shortly after, the architect came back and said he would do it for $75,000. He had a dream telling him to do it. The parish council said okay but the parish said no. They could not afford it and felt Fr. Bernard was using Mary's request as a device to do his own bidding. When Fr. Bernard received about $50,000 in anonymous gifts, the council said to move ahead. Fr. Bernard had promised Fr. Gino not to promote Mary's Shrine and for the next seven years Fr. Bernard lived in poverty to save for the work on the shrine. In 1982 he returned to Rome with a group and to see Fr. Gino. At the meeting Fr. Gino ignored him, as if he didn't even know him. Finally Fr. Bernard left with his group. As he was leaving he decided he had to go and talk to Fr. Gino. At that very moment an assistant to Fr. Gino came up and said he was looking for an American priest. Fr. Bernard said he as one and was told that Fr. Gino wanted to see him. After quite a few moments Fr. Gino told Fr. Bernard the Blessed Mother was not pleased with him. Fr. Bernard almost fell through the floor with disbelief. Fr. Gino said the Blessed Mother was not pleased because he was not telling his parishioners that she was actually present at the Donora Church. Now he does. Fr. Bernard told us that he went in to the Church to say the rosary, but could not do it. He kneeled and prayed for help. He heard a voice "put on your cassock." He was wearing a sweater at the time and could not believe a message from the Blessed Mother would have anything to do with how he was dressed, but as he said, She is a woman and our Mother. He went to his room and put on his cassock and went back to Church. He was at peace and finished his rosary. He prayed for a sign again and was told "look into my eyes." When he looked at the eyes of the painting, he saw the eyes of Mary. She said, "Now you see me."

Father Bernard says that he received a special blessing to heal with his kissed hands, and I was fortunate to have him bless me. If you come to visit, I will take you to the shrine. Fr. Bernard is still not able to promote the shrine since he made that promise to Fr. Gino not to do that.

Love,
Tom

CHAPTER 39

Pleasant Surprises

I had run a 5-minute mile every year until I was fifty years old. It was taking more effort and a longer training time to do it. That year I was fifty, I decided I would not be able to do it because the last several time trials were not getting close to 5 minutes. Then just as I was debating my 5-minute effort, I saw the high school mile group about to start a time trial. I was back about 50 yards. I clicked my stopwatch and took off after them. On the next lap, the coach called out, "Don't let that old guy catch you." On the next lap, he called, "Don't let that old guy pass you." At the final lap, he yelled, "Catch that old guy." A lap later, I clicked my watch for the mile. I had run 4.34. I simply jogged off to my auto and left. At home I was in agony. It took me several days to recover.

This time I decided I would change my sports to tennis and golf.

While at the Allegheny Country Club in Sewickley Heights, Pennsylvania, I played a lot of tennis. Occasionally we needed a fourth for our doubles, and somehow we were fortunate to solicit Trever Heck to play with us. Trevor was a great athlete at Sewickley Academy. He was their top tennis player and top golfer. He certainly was better than we were in tennis. I had won the seniors golf that year so he challenged me to a golf game. Despite the fact that I thought he would slaughter me in golf, we went out for the big match. At the end, Trevor said, "Well, I shot a 74, but you beat me by one stroke." At that time I was seventy-five years old. I never thought I would shoot my age, but to my amazement I did it. I have never come close since that day.

When I was at the Harvard Business School, I was the athletic representative for my section. We played all sports starting with football. My roommate was Byron Campbell, who was a star at Yale. In tennis there was a big final between the former Harvard captain, Dozier Gardiner, and Stephen Kaye, the former Yale captain. They played every year for years, and Gardiner won every year. At the business school, they ended up playing in the finals and Dozier won.

Years later I was on the Board of Trustees for the Arizona Tax Free Fund. The meetings were in Scottsdale and I stayed at John Gardiner's Tennis Ranch. Whom should I meet but Steven Kaye. He seemed excited to see me and told me how he had just played Dozier in the Massachusetts 70 and over, and he had beaten him in the finals. I congratulated him and said I had the afternoon off and would like to play a match with him. Reluctantly he said okay, and we played. I won the match. He said, "Tom that's the shortest time I have felt that good after my great victory over Dozier."

The next year I was staying at the Arizona Biltmore. In 2001 the World Trade Center had been destroyed. The World Series of Baseball was moved out to Arizona. As I got on the elevator, there was a very small old man in a Yankee uniform. I said, "Oh, you are with the Yankees," thinking he was joking around. He said, "Yes, sir, I am." I could tell by the tone of his voice he was sincere. I said to him, "My Dad played on the Yankees." He said, "What was his name?" I said, "Jim Courtney." He said, "Left-handed pitcher," and went out the elevator door. My Dad had died in 1973, thirty years earlier. I found out I had talked to the manager of accommodations for the Yankees. He must have been close to one hundred years old.

Sesquicentennial Dinner at the Met

In 1991 Posy and I attended the Sesquicentennial Celebration of Fordham University. It was held at the New Egypt Room at the Metropolitan Museum. I was seated at a table with a number of my Fordham friends when I heard that Dan Shedrick had given a ten-million-dollar gift to Fordham.

In 1964 I had gone to the Penn Relays to see Fordham teams run. They had two excellent relay teams. I saw Dan Shedrick down on the track and went down to talk to him. I gave him a pep talk and his team won that day. Now I was wondering if my pep talk had been an encouragement to Dan to make such a fine contribution. At that moment, Dan came over to our table and knelt down next to me. He said, "Tom, do you remember the pep talk you gave me at the Penn Relays?"

Then he got up and said, "I would like to introduce my date, Martha Stewart." We exchanged greetings and as they left, Posy asked, "Do you know who Martha Stewart is?" I said, "Yes, she is Dan's date."

CHAPTER 40

Three Sons and Family

My three boys were good athletes and starred on the soccer, basketball, and tennis teams at Sewickley Academy. There was no track team. Tom ran in some AAU races and did well. He went to Princeton, and it was very exciting to see him win on the mile relay team at the Melrose Games. He ran the third leg on the two-mile relay team that won the Ivy Title at the Penn Relays. He went on to the Wharton Business School for his master's. Today he has his own company called the Courtney Group, buying and selling small companies. He and his wife, Vien, have four children: Andrew, Sophie, Nicholas, and Henry. They live in Newport Beach, California.

Andrew Courtney 2000, first Grandchild

Peter, my second son, was a star basketball player and tennis captain at Sewickley Academy. He went to Vanderbilt and took his business degree at Fordham Graduate Business School. Today he is president of Greenwich Investment Management, an investment management firm that specializes in high-yield tax-free municipal bonds. Peter and his wife, Elizabeth, have a daughter, Marielle, and a son, Lyon. They live in Southport, Connecticut.

Frank, our third son, excelled in sports at Sewickley Academy in soccer and was captain of the tennis team. Frank told me he would like to go to Harvard. I told him that he needed to show them he would contribute to the school. He said, "How can I do that?" Frank was a very fast runner with good endurance. I told him that if he could do well in the Pennsylvania Junior Olympics, Harvard would be impressed, particularly since Sewickley had no track team. As soon as the tennis team finished its spring season, with Frank as the captain, he started to practice running on our golf course. He ran two preliminary races to qualify for the 400, and then ran in the Junior Olympic 400 and won. Harvard accepted him. Unfortunately he had some severe leg problems and was unable to continue with his running. Frank went to Harvard and did graduate work at the University of Michigan. Today he works in a specialty metals company, Keystone Manufacturing. Frank and Donna have three girls: Marguerite, Francesca, and Josephine. They live in Sewickley, Pennsylvania.

2011 Christmas in Wyndemere, Naples, Florida.

Between 2000 and this photo a lot of things happened.

Three boys, three wives, nine grandchildren

Tom's 75th Birthday

My Mother's 80th birthday

L to R Brian, Kevin, Tom, Mother, Jim, Dennis

Trivial Pursuit Winners, our team, Naples

L to R bottom row: Jay Ricks, Debby Ricks, Posy, Veora Little,

Back row: Unknown (sore looser?), John
Little, Brent Lambert, Tom

Canoe Race at Family Reunion: L to R Peter, Dad, Tom, Frank

Track as a Professional Sport

Where is track today? I was told last week that Drew Hunter ran 3.57 for the mile. Hunter, who just graduated from high school, turned pro. Adidas signed him to a ten-million-dollar contract.

When I ran track, the motivation was the thrill of competition. I eventually set my objectives and I had goals to break the half-mile world record, which I did, and win gold medals in the Olympics in the 800 meters, the 400 meters, and the 1600-meter relay in the 1956 Melbourne Olympics, which I almost did.

If I went on a European trip, my food and board was provided and we received a daily stipend of $2.00. It was exciting to travel the world.

My hometown of Livingston, New Jersey, was going to raise money to send my Dad to see me run in the Olympics. The Amateur Athletic Union cautioned my Dad that if he took the trip, it might jeopardize my amateur standing. He did not go. That kind of perverse behavior set the stage for professional track. Usain Bolt from Jamaica has made over $25 million a year for the past eight years.

I would have liked to have the opportunity to make a few dollars. But it didn't happen. Wes Santee was punished for taking too much expense money for some of the races he ran. They told him he was no longer an amateur but a professional. He said there was no professional track. And they said, "You are it!" Jim Thorpe, the world's greatest athlete, had to return his medals from the 1912 Olympics because he played in a single semipro baseball game. He was ostracized and only years later did he get some recognition for his tremendous feats.

Did I feel cheated? No, and I am still thankful for the opportunities it gave me. Nothing in life stays the same. We just go on to the next challenge in our life. Things in life happen, and as my parents told us boys, you do the best you can with that you have. With persistence and determination, nothing is impossible. For me that attitude was and still is very important. When adversity showed up and it did, I believed I could overcome it.

Fact Sheet: What Do You Like

Favorite TV shows: My wife and I watch *Jeopardy!* most
                       nights.

Favorite music: I enjoy classical music, and I like to
                       sing.

Favorite books: I read the entire series of the *The 100
                       Greatest Books.*

                       Many of those were wonderful. I enjoy
                       learning and am reading Jean Smith's
                       book on *Eisenhower in War and Peace.*

First car: My first car was a Volvo.

Current car: A Mercedes.

First job: My first job was as a caddy at Cedar
                       Hill Golf Course in Livingston, New
                       Jersey. I was ten years old and was paid
                       seventy-five cents for eighteen holes.
                       That bag was heavy.

Family:	My wife is Margaret although she is nicknamed Posy. My oldest boy, Tom will be fifty-four this year, Peter is fifty-two and Frank is forty-nine. We have nine grandchildren, all are wonderful kids, we think they are exceptional.
Pets:	We had dogs when I was a kid.
Favorite breakfast:	I eat Cheerios every day with blueberries.
Favorite meal:	My favorite meat is prime rib of beef, first cut, rare.
Favorite beverages:	Powerade and wine.
First running memory:	My first running memory was the first half mile inter squad race in high school.
Running heroes:	I knew nothing about running when I started and didn't have any heroes. Heinz Oltzheimer from Germany was a runner I saw race in Madison Square Garden when I was in high school. He was a great runner who ran from the front, and he stunned everyone in the race.
Greatest running moment:	My greatest running moment was the Olympic 800 meters.
Worst running moment:	My worst running moment was as a freshman at Fordham. I made the two-mile relay team and unbeknownst to me

| | I had mononucleosis. We were running at Madison Square Garden, and I ran so poorly that even my own teammate Bill Persicetty asked for new time trials the next Monday. |

Last job: I worked until I was seventy-eight years old and was Chairman of the Boards at Oppenheimer Funds and Chairman of Pimco for some of their funds. They had a mandatory retirement at seventy-five, but being the Chairman I would never let them bring up the subject. Finally at seventy-eight, they merged some of the boards, and I decided to retire. I had a long and interesting business life.

Hobbies/Interests: Today, I play duplicate bridge with Posy at our club, I play tennis and golf. I like to visit family and old friends.

Nicknames: My best nickname is on my license plate and it says "T Court." I was called the "Fordham Flash" after the Olympics and at a celebratory dinner at Leone's Restaurant, legendary baseball player Frankie Frisch got up and said "I am the 'Fordham Flash." I told the press that was his nickname, he earned it, and we should let him have it.

An Investment Club Talk at Allegheny Country Club, June 20, 1996

T he following is a talk I gave to an investment club at the Allegheny Country Club. I thought it might be interesting to you.

Tom Courtney has an economics degree from Fordham University and an MBA from Harvard. He started his analytical work at Kidder Peabody. He came out to Pittsburgh in 1975 as president of Federated Investment Counseling, where he worked until Federated sold out to Aetna in 1982. Since then he worked in Venture Capital, and heads up his own investment firm, Courtney Associates.

Tom is on twenty-six boards, including ones for the Hawaiian Trust Company, Arizona, and is chairman of Pimco VIT Funds and chairman of Oppenheimer Funds, which included the Rochester Funds. He was a director of the Financial Analysts Federation and is a Chartered Financial Analyst.

How Does the Presidential Election Affect the Stock Market?

I asked Charlotte, "How long do I have to talk?" She said, "It's your job to talk and our job to listen. If we finish before you, we will let you know." Always remember you are unique . . . just like everyone else!

Actually I am like the sixth husband of Liz Taylor. I know what is expected of me, but I'm not sure I can make it *interesting.*

Chart 1 shows the four-year cycle. The stock market *bottoms* occur approximately two years before each election year. The Dow Jones has gone up from 3800 in January '95 to a high of 5800 in May of '96. If the Fed continues to ease money, the market will probably continue to move higher before November 4.

Chart 2 shows you investments over the long term. Stocks have returned more than long-term government bonds, and short US Treasury bills have outpaced inflation. Does that mean the best investment is always stocks?

Please look at Chart 3. It shows the DJIA on the bottom and the compounded rate of return for DJIA stocks on the top. Notice what happens every time the compounded rate of return of the DJIA stocks reached an extremely positive level. Almost exactly ten years following each stock market extreme, the compounded rate of return was close to O or negative.

For the last fifteen years the stock market has been regarded as a safe harbor; however, as you can see, the return on stocks has currently reached another historic extreme that will probably "return to normal" over the next ten years.

Economists and accountants come up with all these charts. I'd like to talk about economists.

- An economist will tell you 1,000 ways to make love, but he doesn't know any women.
- I asked a CPA what he did—he said he didn't understand the question.
- One useless man is a waste—two is a law firm.
- A woman went to a doctor. He told her she was crazy. She said she wanted another opinion. "Okay you are also ugly!"
- Two psychiatrists met. One said, "You're fine, how am I?"

A classmate of mine from the Harvard Business School was running a small growth stock fund for Bankers Trust. He had a good ten-year performance record when we had lunch in 1972. The funds assets were close to $1.5 billion, which was a lot in those days. I asked him how he would handle a bad market and a run on his fund. He said no problem. He owned over 300 different stocks in diversified industries and had good liquidity. The market collapsed in 1973 and 1974. His fund went down 38 percent in 1973 and 54 percent in 1974 and assets dropped to below $200 million. Meanwhile he switched jobs to another fund group, who were impressed with his ten-year record. Later he told me that the 300 stocks all behaved like one stock and it was next to impossible to sell them.

One has to wonder today what would happen if something upset the market. What would happen if Iraq or one of those extremist groups nuclear-bombed New York City. With computerized trading and the trillion dollars that has gone into the mutual funds in the last two years, it wouldn't surprise me to see the market go off to 3000 to 4000 points in a week. I am not predicting such a thing, but it is important to understand that it could happen. The market is in a high-risk period. If you own any of these high-tech stocks, like Amati Communications that has gone up 1651 percent in the past twelve months, maybe you should be building some cash reserves.

To balance those risks, I would like to look at what's in the works for the future. I am going to give you twelve different areas.

1. Nanotechnology—a new science that allows researchers to manipulate individual atoms. Japanese scientists have recently built the world's smallest car, complete with headlights, a windshield, and bumpers, and it's no bigger than a grain of rice. Macro-machines will soon be built particle by particle.

2. Prototyping—an Israeli firm is in the early stages of a new kind of prototyping—the atom, by atom duplication of solid objects.

3. Personal Communication Service—licenses are being auctioned off at this time. PCS will eventually be less expensive than your own phone—you can carry it anywhere in the world, you will have your own number, that you can keep no matter where you live, for life. IBM is a leader in this area.

4. Cellular biology—we will have cures for cancer, heart disease, baldness, shortness, and tallness. Merck is a good example. This week several drug companies announced they had new combination drugs that helped AIDS victims.

5. Medical technology—there are several companies working on a technology that will allow a skilled vascular surgeon to stitch a vital-vein from 2000 miles away. Intuitive Surgical leads in this area.

6. Translation—researchers at Carnegie Mellon have developed a language translation system. The computer digitizes your words, and a voice synthesizes a translated version, and it is to be no bigger than a phone. I suppose this could be tricky. I saw where a Russian translator translated "The spirit is willing, but the flesh is weak" to "The whiskey is fine, but the meat is spoiled."

7. New security measures—pulse and laser weapons that stun and disorient people are being developed. Long-range combustion inhibitors will be able to cut the engines of speeding vehicles. Companies that encrypt data and provide security will profit.

8. New auto advances—today, electric cars are being promoted, but toxic materials in the batteries are a major problem. American Flywheel Systems has developed an electromechanical battery that solves the problem and takes a car 600 miles on a charge. New technology will make autos at 1/3 the weight of steel cars. It will be molded and it will cut the number of parts by 90 percent. Electrics are expected to get up to 300 miles to a charge.

9. Sniff detectors—Neotronics has developed a computer-governed network that can detect differences in smells. It could be used to sniff drugs, test food spoilage, and detect the shipment of international weapons.

10. Air pollution—noise cancellation technologies have developed a way to measure sound waves and create their opposites—they cancel each other out. The result is silence. Great for noise pollution—silent armies, silent airplanes, silent autos.

11. Plant genetics—Mycogen has developed a strain of corn that resists pests. No more spraying, no more chemicals. Monsanto is the innovator here.

12. Cyberspace—Compact has gone up 6777 percent since 1984, but the high-tech boom is just starting. The cyber network, the Internet, is just taking off. There is *a new nation* called cyberspace— it's already populated with brilliant oddballs that like to communicate at 3 in the morning. Netscape stock tripled since its offering, and it is selling at a capitalized value of $5 billion—and not yet making profits.

So what we see is that we are in the early stages of a long-term boom. Capital spending is surging and world trade is leading the way. Actually capital spending in the computer area is vastly understated. The government doesn't count spending in software, which in 1996 will be $75 billion. Microsoft has a major lead. Only 25 percent of homes have computers, while 98 percent have phones and televisions. But you can already install a card into the computer to turn it into a TV, and using the Internet, you can call anywhere in the world and talk for a dollar an hour. We can go directly from the computer to the printer, and soon from computer to computer.

The largest two industries in the world are autos and oil. Think what the new changes I spoke about will do to these industries.

Even the government is getting its act together. True, the so-called Republican Revolution is just a slowdown in spending growth, but no matter who gets in, it won't be on programs of vast new spending increases because both parties have been forced to move to the right because that's what people like us are demanding.

Now My Forecast: They say economists tell it like it is. A guy had a pussycat and was gone for two weeks. He asked his friend, who was an economist, to take care of his cat. When he returned, he asked, "How is my pussycat?" The other economist said, "He died." The first economist said, "Don't be so direct. Ease into it. For example, say the pussycat was on the roof and he fell off. By the way, how is my Mother? Well, she was on the roof . . ."

Forecasting is difficult, especially if it's about the future. However, you know one thing about having an inconsiderable reputation— you can afford to squander it.

We are in a historic extreme level for return on stocks, but we are in the early stages of the technology boom. We will have a major collapse in the market in the next year, but it won't destroy our technology boom, and if you can ride through it, you will be okay.

My portfolio would be as follows

> 20% cash
> 20% real estate
> 20% muni bonds
> 40% stocks < 20% growth issues, < 20% value issues of that total, half of that is international, and about 8% in gold stocks.

Why gold? It doesn't disappear, it's always there, and we will see a shortage in the near future. There have been 3.6 billion ounces produced since the pharaohs. If you melted it in a cube, it would fit in the ice rink at the Civic Center. It's a little more than 1/2 ounce per person. Central banks have been heavy sellers—500 tons in 1993, but they are running out. The way to play it is stocks. If gold goes from $385 to $500 an ounce, you make 30 percent profit, but the mining company that is today making a profit of $20 an ounce will jump to $135 an ounce = a 670 percent increase and the stocks will triple. Gold funds have had a mediocre performance for the past ten years while gold went nowhere. They should be spectacular performers when the metal takes off. Newmont Mining is a leader.

I would like to comment on one other area. If you take your $1.2 million marital deduction, put it in a crummy trust for your children, buy a second to die insurance policy. Your children, depending on their ages, could end up with close to $10 million with no taxes to be paid. If you have to earn an equivalent amount before you die, when you consider you must pay 40 percent taxes as it's earned, 40 percent taxes as it accumulates, and 60 percent to 70 percent on death taxes, you would have to earn about $40 million to duplicate the $10 million after taxes.

An economist who had a drinking problem was told by his wife if he came home drunk, she would put him out. Sure enough, he went to an investment club meeting and got drunk. He tried to sneak in the house, but tripped on the rug and fell on his wife's favorite vase in the living room. She turned on the lights. He looked up and said, "I'm going to dispense with my prepared remarks, and go right to the questions—any questions?"

What are the stocks you like right now?

ACR Group (75 cents OTC) = distribution of heating, air conditioning, refrigerator equipment, and supplies. Sales have gone from 13 to 25, 30, 41, 56 in the past five years and the company has sacrificed earnings for sales. In five years it hopes to have sales over $200 million, earn 5 to 10 percent or $1.00 to $2.00 a share. They intend to sell out or have a stock in the $10 to $15 range.

Walden Residential - REIT $20.00 OTC – 9 percent yield, growing at 9 percent in residential apartments.

Long-term holdings - own the leaders in the areas I mentioned.

How Far Can a Bear Run and How Fast

I am putting this chapter in my book because my granddaughter, Francesca, loved the story of a bear chasing Grandpa Tom.

Posy and I were in Arizona for some board meetings, and we decided we would visit Valer Clark Austin. Albie Gordon and Valer had divorced, and Valer had remarried Josiah Austin. I hoped it would give me a chance to see my goddaughter, Valerie. They lived next to the Mexican border and the Coronado National Park. While Posy was getting together with Valer, I decided to take a walk. I walked about a mile from the house, admiring the spacious views of the park.

Suddenly I saw a bear in the distance. For a moment that was exciting, until I saw the bear was jogging toward me. Now I became a little nervous. I reversed my path and started to jog back to the house. As I increased my pace, the bear increased his pace. I had never run against a bear, and the idea sent chills up my spine. I now thought how fast a bear can run and how far can he run. He was gaining on me when I decided to take off. The bear decided the same and he took off. For about a half mile, we were both in a fast race and the bear was winning. What could I do—only go a little faster, and I knew I couldn't last much longer. I looked back and the bear slowed his pace and stopped. I went into a jog and was very happy to make it to the house.

CHAPTER 45

Persistence and Determination

Bob Mackin—a close friend of mine, a track teammate at Fordham, and an author friend—asked me, What is the thrust of your story?

I mentioned the quote from Elder Sterling W. Sill that was taped on our refrigerator in Livingston. It provided motivation for the brothers. It went as follows: "The average man's complacent when he's done his best to score. But the champion does his best, and then he does a little more."

There was another clipping on that same refrigerator that had a tremendous impact on me. Calvin Coolidge's quote on persistence. It said, "Press on. Nothing in the world can take the place of persistence, talent will not: nothing is more common than unsuccessful men with talent. Genius will not: unrewarded genius is almost a proverb. Education alone will not: the world is full of educated derelicts. Persistence and determination are omnipotent."

This particular quote made a dramatic difference in my life. I can't tell you how often I stopped and reread it. It helped me to focus on my goals. My parents had taught the brothers to do the best you can with what you have. They impressed us that we had an obligation to continue to try to do better. God gave us gifts, and we were to use those gifts.

Sports mirrors life. God gave us emotions, and they sustain us in our life. With persistence and determination, I was able to accept defeat. I was able to learn from those defeats. I knew what it took to achieve my goals. The answer is never give up. You will surprise yourself with what you can achieve. I know that in the Olympic 800 meters, I gave everything I had.

How do I sum it up? Think positively. Be bold and courageous. You never know what you can accomplish until you try it. Even then if you try and are unsuccessful, you go back and try again. Never give in. Persistence and determination have always solved the problems of the world. In life you are given opportunities, and you must take advantage of them. You must do your best. Believe you will succeed—never give in!

2018, Posy and Tom with Grandchildren